THE TRIAL OF JESUS

✠

THE
TRIAL
OF
JESUS

✠ ✠ ✠

Alan Watson

✠

The University of Georgia Press
ATHENS & LONDON

© 1995 by the University of Georgia Press
Athens, Georgia 30602
All rights reserved

Designed by Kathi L. Dailey
Set in Aldus and Optima by Tseng Information Systems, Inc.
Printed and bound by Thomson-Shore
The paper in this book meets the guidelines for permanence and
durability of the Committee on Production Guidelines for
Book Longevity of the Council on Library Resources.

Printed in the United States of America

99 98 97 96 95   c   5 4 3 2 1

Library of Congress Cataloging in Publication Data
Watson, Alan.
The trial of Jesus / Alan Watson.
p.   cm.
Includes bibliographical references and index.
ISBN 0-8203-1717-9 (alk. paper)
1. Jesus Christ—Trial. 2. Passion narratives (Gospels)   I. Title.
BT440.W27   1995
232.96′2—dc20   94-39088
British Library Cataloging in Publication Data available

✠

CONTENTS

✠ ✠ ✠

✠

PREFACE

✠ ✠ ✠

THIS IS A BOOK THAT I HAVE WANTED TO WRITE FOR more than three decades, ever since I read, and was moved but not entirely persuaded by, Paul Winter's brilliant *On the Trial of Jesus.* The problems brought about by contradictions in the main sources seemed to put any convincing solution of the course of events out of the question. I started to make progress only after I had written on the narrative in John's Gospel in my *Jesus and the Jews: The Pharisaic Tradition in John.* Two contradictions in that Gospel stand out. First, John is much more anti-Jewish than the Synoptics, yet of all the Gospels it is the most sympathetic to the Jews: only in John does the entirely wonderful Pharisee, Nicodemus, appear; only in John are the Jewish leaders shown as justified in seeking Jesus' death because, if he continued to act as he was doing, the Romans would come and destroy Jerusalem (or the Temple) and the nation; only in John do the Jewish leaders not mock Jesus on the cross. Second, John shows great knowledge of conditions in Palestine but can also make enormous gaffes: three times the Gospel states that the high priest was appointed for a year. How can this be?

The answer lies in the nature of a composite work, and unless John is the work of John the son of Zebedee (as few believe), the Gospel is a composite. Thus, hostility to the Jews comes from one strand in the Gospel, the contradictory sympathetic picture from another. The understanding of Palestinian conditions comes from one strand, the gaffes from another. Responsibility for the gaffes lies on the final redactor—he had the last chance to put them right—so credit for understanding must go to an earlier tradition. To this subject I will return briefly in chapter 3.

That the evangelist might have had little understanding of Palestine enables us to think again about the claim in John 18.31 that the Sanhedrin was not allowed to put people to death. That verse is the only solid-looking evidence for the proposition. If we regard it, even temporarily, as possibly dubious, we see that the evidence to the contrary is overwhelming. Without that verse no one (I believe) would have doubted that the Sanhedrin could have executed Jesus. Even with that verse a large proportion of scholars believe on balance that the Sanhedrin had the power to put Jews to death.

But if we can believe that in all probability the Sanhedrin had the power to put Jews to death for some offenses against religion, we can examine the trial and the events leading up to it with fresher eyes. And the key to understanding the course of events will be the answer to the question, Why did the Sanhedrin not execute Jesus?

Because this book is not a commentary but attempts to be explanatory, I have, with clarity and simplicity as my goals, seen no reason to cite all modern authorities—in any event an impossible task—but only those that bear directly pro or con on my thesis. My hesitations in following this course—in any event a practice I have used before—were much reduced by the 1994 publication of Raymond E. Brown's very useful compendium,

The Death of the Messiah, which covers much of the action that I deal with. Again, following my common practice, I stick as closely as I am able to the texts, what *they* say, while examining their plausibility. I eschew the ever-fashionable approach of knowing what must have been and altering the evidence to fit.[1]

I should emphasize at the outset—and it can scarcely be too strongly emphasized—that what the Gospels deal with are *traditions* about Jesus. The Gospels are not written by eyewitnesses, nor do they attempt to set out the course of Jesus' life as modern biographies would. Accordingly, my search for what happened in the events leading up to Jesus' trial and the trial itself is a search not primarily for historical truth but for the most plausible tradition.

The reader will notice repetitions or apparent repetitions in this book. They are, I believe, inevitable. Though in no sense have I written as if I were reporting a modern trial, there are similarities. There are four main witnesses: Matthew, Mark, Luke, and John. They must first be examined separately for consistency. Then, they must be tested against one another for plausibility overall and in detail. But in contrast to the examination of modern witnesses, in a book like this parts of the testimony of a Gospel may be left aside, to be brought up later. The same episode may also be examined more than once from different standpoints. At various stages there can be—and there is—a partial summing up of the evidence, to help build up the case later. Even the last chapter, which may resemble an attorney's closing statement, contains evidence not adduced before.

Translations from the New Testament are either my own or those in the *New Oxford Annotated Bible,* 2nd edition (New York, 1991); from Josephus and Philo mainly those in the Loeb Classical Library; from the Mishnah those by Herbert Danby, *The Mishnah.*

ACKNOWLEDGMENTS

TO MY GREAT BENEFIT, A NUMBER OF FRIENDS READ drafts of this book: Leigh Bauer, Calum Carmichael, Paul Finkelman, Steven F. Friedell, Olivia Robinson, Alyssa Ward. Numerous drafts were typed cheerfully and very efficiently by Sherri Mauldin. The staff of the University of Georgia law library were unfailingly helpful. I am much in the debt of all of them. Their varying skills have much improved my product.

I dedicate this book to some remarkable scholars, friends all of them, who taught me by example. Among the characteristics they share is a passionate wholehearted love of scholarship, love of humankind, and love of life. I will never cease to be grateful for the ways in which they enhance my life.

THE TRIAL OF JESUS

✟

INTRODUCTION

✟ ✟ ✟

THE TRIAL OF JESUS IS THE MOST MOMENTOUS AND fateful in western history. But what happened? An axiom of ancient historians is that where we have one account of something we know everything that occurred, where we have more than one account we know nothing. But here we have four accounts in the Gospels, and the divergences are great, especially between John and the Synoptics. Not surprisingly, scholars differ in their interpretations. Again, I must emphasize that in this case what we must search for is not so much historical truth as the most plausible tradition.

The main questions that must be answered to evaluate the arrest, trial or trials, and execution of Jesus are well known and, indeed, obvious. What events led to the arrest? Which groups were hostile to Jesus, and why? What was Jesus' response to the hostility? Who arrested Jesus? Was Jesus tried by the Sanhedrin? If so, why? If so, on what charge? Could the Sanhedrin impose the death penalty? Was Jesus tried by Pontius Pilate? If so, on what charge? If Pilate tried Jesus, did he regard him as innocent and condemn him nonetheless? If so, why? Who crucified Jesus?

The ultimate hope for a book of this kind should be to establish what did happen, at least in outline. But that cannot be achieved. So the main goal has to be limited to attaining historical plausibility according to the traditions. We have four accounts. I do not believe we can make progress by choosing from each of them those episodes and elements that are to our liking. Such an approach would inevitably lead to some or much arbitrariness. Rather, each Gospel should be examined separately and tested at the outset for self-consistency, then subsequently for plausibility against information from other sources. We have four accounts, but since I accept the common opinion that in some measure Matthew and Luke derive from Mark, we can partly restrict our study to Mark and John. And, at the beginning stage, we should not bolster arguments about Mark by appeals to Matthew and Luke. A search for plausibility is different from a search for truth. More than one account may be wholly plausible, but not more than one may be totally true. The choices for truth are (1) none is true, (2) one is true, (3) some accounts are partly true, partly false, and (4) all accounts are partly true, partly false.

The Gospels are based on preexisting sources, whether oral or written, and the redactors were tied to the tradition. Each Gospel writer would be selective, could excise unpalatable elements, and could change the emphasis and even the theological message, but he could not invent the tradition afresh. His audience knew too much.

The Gospels were set down in, and for, particular communities, and they will have tendencies that result from the circumstances in which they were written. This must be emphasized before we trace the events set out in Mark and John, though the impact of these tendencies will not be discussed until chapter 11. Thus, there is widespread agreement that Mark was written in the 60s A.D. at Rome. If this is correct, then the redactor would have been faced with the embarrassing fact that his god, Jesus, was put to death in a brutal way, apparently for treason, by the Romans as an occupying force. The embarrassment would be all the more because at that time many or most of the Christians in Rome would not be Roman citizens. We might expect that Mark would shift the blame elsewhere, as far as possible. Of course, this could be true wherever Mark was written, provided it was within the Roman empire. The tendencies in John might be other. I have argued in *Jesus and the Jews* that at the root of John's narratives there is a Pharisaic source—which I designate as S—that was anti-Christian. That source and tradition were too well known in the community to be ignored, and John had to deal with them. By small and subtle changes in the narrative John defanged the Pharisaic tradition and superimposed his theological message. But the S tradition still shines through. On this basis we might expect this Gospel rather to underplay the role of Jewish leaders in Jesus' death. Yet at the same time the redactor is the most virulently anti-Jewish of the four Gospel writers. Fortunately for me, in the present context I scarcely rely on my previous arguments. Still, it will be appropriate for me to say a little in chapter 3 about my understanding of this Pharisaic tradition.

A fundamental assumption of mine for this book must be made explicit. When a relatively lengthy work is a composite, with the author working from earlier sources and traditions, then the sources used will leave some traces no matter how they have been manipulated. If the redactor uses a source that opposes his viewpoint but has to be dealt with because it is embedded in the tradition, then no matter how much he changes the emphasis, the nature of the source will shine through in some places. The corollary is that if there is no indication in a Gospel of a particular tendency, then we cannot simply imagine that the tendency must have been there and emend the texts to fit. For example in the present context, if either Mark or John had used a source that portrayed Jesus as a patriot revolutionary against Roman occupation, some trace of this source would, I believe, remain in the Gospel despite the best efforts of the redactor to clear the record.

The arrest, trial, and execution of Jesus show many facets, and it is the beginning of wisdom to realize that we need not study all of them exhaustively. Thus, the role of the Sanhedrin is central. It is important that both Pharisees and Sadducees sat on that court, but we need not for our purposes establish the proportions of each group. We must decide whether the trial at night was legal or not, but we need not decide how many judges were required for conviction. We need to know whether the Sanhedrin could impose the death penalty and whether death by stoning was the appropriate punishment, but we need not inquire whether all four forms of execution discussed in the Mishnah Sanhedrin were then in use nor exactly how each was carried out.

1

✛

THE
HISTORICAL
BACKGROUND

✛ ✛ ✛

DURING JESUS' LIFETIME, AND BEFORE AND AFTER, messianism was a powerful call among the Jews.[1] And messianism is a major theme of this book. When we discuss it briefly for the career of Jesus, we must avoid one error at all costs: to uncover the nature of the Messiah in the Jewish tradition of that day, we must not use as evidence the New Testament or Jewish materials composed after the death of Jesus. The reason is obvious. If Jesus comes to be regarded in any way as the Messiah, or as somehow connected with the Messiah, or as the king of the Jews, then his image will have an impact on the subsequent characterization of the Messiah or the king of the Jews. The issues that really concern us—though, as it happens, they need not be addressed directly and at length in this book—are twofold. Did Jesus have characteristics that caused people to believe he could be the Messiah? If so, what did these people expect of him?

We need not discuss the views held before the time of Jesus that were obsolete in his day, but we must not forget that the views on the nature of the Messiah were various. We must consider both those traditions about the Messiah that could give rise to a belief during Jesus' life that he might possibly be the Messiah, or connected with him, and those traditions that would indicate he could not be a messianic figure.

A first source is the Jewish Bible book of Malachi,[2] which is much about the coming of the Lord. Malachi 4.5 reports that the prophet Elijah will be sent as a forerunner:

> Lo, I will send you the prophet Elijah before the great and terrible day of the Lord comes. 6. He will turn the hearts of parents to their children and the hearts of children to their parents, so that I will not come and strike the land with a curse.

It will be recalled that in Matthew 17.10–13. Jesus said that Elijah had come, and his disciples thought he meant John the Baptist.[3] Some people, indeed, thought Jesus was Elijah.[4]

A second source for the Messiah, the Psalms of Solomon—which did not win a place in accepted Scripture—seems to have been composed very probably in Jerusalem, around the time of Pompey the Great, perhaps shortly after his death in 48 B.C.[5] Psalm 17 is most relevant for us. Emil Schürer rightly points out that Psalm 17 indicates the longing for the Messiah of a people who had fallen under Roman rule. God himself is king of Israel:

> 17.1. Lord, you yourself are our king for ever and ever,
> For in you shall our soul glory.

God chooses David as king:

> 17.4. You, O Lord, chose David king over Israel,
> And you swore to him concerning his seed for ever,
> That his kingship would never fail before you.

But foreigners have usurped the kingdom (17.5ff.). God will send a king from the house of David to destroy the godless nations. The king will assemble the holy people, he will settle them in Israel according to their tribes, and he will allow no strangers to dwell among them:

17.21. Behold, O Lord, and raise up unto them their king,
      the son of David,
  At the time you have [fore]seen, O God, to rule over
      Israel your servant.
  22. And gird him with strength, to shatter unrighteous
      rulers,
  Purge Jerusalem from the nations that trample [her]
      in destruction.
  23. With wisdom, with righteousness to drive out
      sinners from the inheritance,
  To destroy the arrogance of the sinner as a potter's
      vessels.
  24. With a rod of iron to shatter all their substance,
  To destroy the godless nations with the word of his
      mouth,
  25. [So that] at his threat nations will flee from his
      presence,
  And to reprove sinners with the thought of their
      heart.
  26. He will assemble a holy people that he will lead in
      righteousness
  And he will judge the tribes of the people made holy
      by the Lord its God.
  27. He will not allow unrighteousness to encamp in their
      midst any longer,
  Nor will dwell with them any man who knows evil.
  For he will know them, that all are sons of their God.

28. And he will divide them according to their tribes
    upon the land,
    And neither sojourner nor alien will dwell with them
    any more.
29. He will judge peoples and nations in the wisdom of
    his righteousness.
30. And he will have the peoples of the nations to serve
    him under his yoke;
    And he will glorify the Lord in the sight of the whole
    earth,
    And he will purify Jerusalem by holiness as of old.
31. [So that] nations will come from the end of the earth
    to see his glory,
    Bringing as gifts her sons who are exhausted.

Thus, for the author of the Psalms of Solomon, the Messiah will descend from David's line, he will save Jerusalem from the foreign dominators and will destroy them, he will bring back the dispersed to Israel, and he will settle the tribes upon the land.

A further source, the third Jewish Sibylline Oracle—also not scriptural—is a composite work, certainly of Egyptian provenance. The main oracle, which alone we will look at, was probably written around 163–145 B.C. [6] God will send a king who, following God's wishes, will stop wars:

652. And then God will send a King from the sun who will stop the entire earth from evil war, killing some, imposing oaths of loyalty on others; and he will not do all these things by his private plans but in obedience to the noble teachings of the great God.

Other kings will launch an attack against Israel and seek to destroy the Temple (663ff.). God will bring great destruction on the earth (669ff.), but the people of God will find salvation:

702. But the sons of the great God will all live peacefully around the Temple, rejoicing in these things which the Creator, just judge and sole ruler, will give. For he alone will shield them, standing by them magnificently as if he had a wall of blazing fire round about. They will be free from war in towns and country. No hand of evil war, but rather the Immortal himself and the hand of the Holy One will be fighting for them. And then all islands and cities will say,

"How much the Immortal loves those men!
heaven, divinely driven sun and moon"
(but the all-bearing earth will be shaken in those days).

The Gentiles will then send gifts to the Temple and ponder the Law (715ff.).[7]

Closely linked with the idea of the Messiah, as we saw especially from the seventeenth Psalm of Solomon, was the notion that the dispersed of Israel would return.[8]

Messianism in the time of Jesus must be set in its historical context. Civil war broke out in Judaea in 63 B.C. between Hyrcanus and Aristobulus. Who these leaders were, their background and aspirations, are matters of little direct relevance for this volume, but their war caused or enabled the Roman general Pompeius Magnus to intervene, and that on the side of Hyrcanus.[9] One of Hyrcanus's allies was Antipater, who was the father of King Herod the Great, who had been born in the late seventies. Antipater forced Aristobulus to retreat to the Temple mount in Jerusalem, and after a three-month siege Pompey captured the Temple. He installed Hyrcanus as high priest and made Judaea a tributary of Rome. Pompey did not annex the territory for Rome but placed it under the supervision of the governor of Syria.

Pompey's interference in the office of high priest is not surprising. It was the highest Jewish political office as well as the most important position in Jewish religious life. Thereafter, the Romans appointed the high priests, theoretically for life but, in reality, according to Roman pleasure.

Antipater had been a Roman supporter even earlier. He had acted as mediator between them and the Nabateans, and had negotiated the reparations that the latter had to pay. Antipater was from an aristocratic Idumaean family who had converted to Judaism. His policy, and that subsequently of his son Herod, was to recognize the Roman might and show unswerving loyalty. He held office under Gabinius, who was governor of Syria from 57 to 54, and when Julius Caesar defeated Pompey, Antipater raised troops to fight for Caesar. When he was in Syria in 47, Caesar appointed Antipater epitropos (overseer) of Judaea, and he gave Herod and his family Roman citizenship. Antipater appointed Herod governor of Galilee. Antipater was murdered in 42. Jewish aristocrats tried to have Herod removed, but his loyalty and that of his father to Rome persuaded the Romans to support him. Still, eventually the Hasmonean Antigonus together with Parthian invaders drove out both the Romans and Herod. Herod went to Rome, where he was formally crowned king of Judaea. In 37, after two years of war in which he enjoyed the enormous support of the Romans, Herod took over the kingdom. He reigned until 4 B.C.

Herod was unpopular in various quarters: the family was only recently Jewish; he had the title of king, which Jews associated with the family of David, to which he certainly did not belong; his rise was connected with the fall of the Hasmonean dynasty; the pace of hellenism was increasing; and he was supported by, and identified with, the Romans. In addition, he was arrogant and cruel—to say the least—in his insecurity.[10] Still, so long as he reigned, the Jews were spared what they regarded as the full indignity of foreign rule. They were not insulted by the presence of a foreign occupying army, they paid taxes to Herod, not to the Romans, and the Jews did not have to use Roman coinage with its graven images and pagan deities. Throughout his reign, Herod was active in building, notably the rebuilding of the Temple in Jerusalem.

By codicils to his last will, Herod appointed his son Archelaus king; named another son, Herod Antipas, as tetrarch of Galilee; and gave Trachonitis and neighboring districts to a third son, Philip.[11] He gave the Roman emperor Augustus power over the ratification of the will,[12] a move intended to secure enforcement. Trouble immediately broke out at Jerusalem.[13] Archelaus went to Rome, and his claim to kingship was challenged by Herod Antipas on the basis that he was king under the will and the will prevailed over the codicils. Varus, the Roman governor of Syria, who in the meantime had entered Jerusalem with three legions, departed leaving one legion there. Sabinus, who was the Roman imperial finance officer of Syria, went to Jerusalem to take charge of Herod's property. The people there consequently rioted and besieged the legion. Guerilla warfare then broke out in various places in Judaea, Samaria, and Galilee, under several leaders including Judas, the son of Ezechias who was noted as a brigand chief and/or opponent of Herod's tyranny.[14] Varus reentered Jerusalem with his two other legions and was successful there and elsewhere. He crucified around two thousand of the worst offenders. Augustus at Rome gave his decision on the will: Archelaus as ethnarch received Idumaea, Judaea, and Samaria; Herod Antipas as tetrarch Peraea and Galilee, Philip as tetrarch Batanaea, Trachonitis, and Auranitis.[15] Archelaus proved to be an incompetent ruler, and in A.D. 6 Augustus deposed him and brought Idumaea, Judaea, and Samaria under direct Roman rule as part of the province of Syria.[16] Accordingly, for the time that concerns us, the lifetime of Jesus, Judaea and Samaria were part of a Roman province under direct military rule; Galilee was not a province but was ruled by the Jewish tetrarch, who was a client of the Romans.[17]

A particular indication of Roman interest in, and control over, the office of high priest is that his vestments were kept in a stone chamber in the Roman fortress, the Antonia, under a triple seal of the priests, temple officials, and the commander of the Roman garrison, and they were released for festivals.[18] According to the historian Josephus, the Romans wanted to be masters of the sacred robe. The custom in fact predated the Roman rule and apparently originated under Herod. It ended in A.D. 36 when Vitellius succeeded Pontius Pilate.[19] Since the Romans did not interfere with the practice of Jewish religion, their purpose involved some sort of political control.[20] The high priest had to wear the robe on particular occasions: thus, the Romans in effect controlled whether these occasions could be held.

In A.D. 6 Augustus sent Quirinius, a consular, to take a census of property in Syria for tax purposes.[21] The Jews were shocked, but their anger was at first restrained by the Sadducean high priest, Joazar. Here we have an indication of Sadducean collaboration with the Roman occupying power. But full revolt broke out under the leadership of Judas from Gamala with the help of Saddok, who was a Pharisee. The tax assessment amounted to putting the Jews in the position of slaves, they claimed, and they wanted the nation to make a bid for independence. Heaven would help them "all the more if with high devotion in their hearts they stood firm and did not shrink from the bloodshed that might be necessary."[22] The revolt failed, but it set the scene for recurring outbreaks in which common features were fierce Jewish national pride, defense of their religion, and abhorrence of paying a foreign tax.

Josephus, the historian who was born around A.D. 37, was a man of complicated belief and background. He was Jewish, a Pharisee in fact, and was put in command of Galilee by the Sanhedrin during the revolt against the Romans. He was captured, but his life was spared. He settled in Rome, became a Roman citizen, and received a pension.

Josephus claims that from the earliest times the Jews had three philosophies with regard to their traditions: that of the Pharisees, of the Sadducees, and of the Essenes. Now Judas and Saddok, he says, started a fourth school of philosophy.[23] This is presumably a reference to those people subsequently called Zealots. Josephus is not saying that all of the Jewish people belonged to one or another of these four groups. He is claiming only that there were four philosophies relating to Jewish traditions. Many Jews, we may assume, were not much given to one tradition or another, and they were relatively lax in their observance: the 'am-ha'aretz, the people of the land. Nor were the philosophies always mutually exclusive. Certainly, one could not easily be at the same time a Pharisee and a Sadducee. But like Saddok, one could be a Pharisee and a Zealot.

Josephus is not to be accepted as an impartial witness. His pro-Roman stance is admitted on all sides. Also, he gives a hellenistic cast to Jewish life, and we should downplay his insistence that the differences between Jewish groups were a matter of philosophical schools.

Josephus is hostile to the Zealots, whom he blames for the destruction of the Temple in A.D. 70. All the more important is it to notice that not only does he claim that the Zealots had a school of philosophy but that it was a philosophy of Jewish traditions. The religious basis of the objection to paying the tax should be stressed. In another place Josephus says of the same Judas from Gamala that he "incited his countrymen to revolt, upbraiding them as cowards for consenting to pay tribute to the Romans and tolerating mortal masters, after having God as their lord."[24] God had blessed the Israelites and settled them in the land of Canaan under a covenant by which they were to serve him alone. To pay taxes to the Romans was to accept them also as lords and to breach the covenant with God.

For our purposes we need not decide whether the term *Zealot* is appropriate for Jesus' day, or even whether we should see organized revolutionaries at that time against the Romans.[25] It is enough to know that after A.D. 6 there were frequent, serious outbreaks of violence, motivated on the Jewish side by religious fervor even more than by a desire for political freedom. Pontius Pilate, as the Roman procurator, had good reason to believe that trouble could easily start if religious passions were aroused. It should be remembered that, according to Josephus, Herod Antipas feared that John the Baptist's religious outpourings would lead to rioting, and he arrested John in a preemptive strike.[26] If people came to regard Jesus as the Messiah in some sense, they would expect from him, as we have already seen, some violent military maneuver against the Romans.

Josephus gives a short description of the Pharisees (of whom, as I have mentioned, he himself was one):

> *Jewish Antiquities* 18.12. The Pharisees simplify their standard of living, making no concession to luxury. They follow the guidance of that which their doctrine has selected and transmitted as good, attaching the chief importance to the observance of those commandments which it has seen fit to dictate to them. They show respect and deference to their elders, nor do they rashly presume to contradict their proposals. 13. Though they postulate that everything is brought about by fate, still they do not deprive the human

will of the pursuit of what is in man's power, since it was God's good pleasure that there should be a fusion and that the will of man with his virtue and vice should be admitted to the council-chamber of fate. 14. They believe that souls have power to survive death and that there are rewards and punishments under the earth for those who have led lives of virtue or vice: eternal imprisonment is the lot of evil souls, while the good souls receive an easy passage to a new life. Because of these views they are, as a matter of fact, extremely influential among the townsfolk; 15. and all prayers and sacred rites of divine worship are performed according to their exposition. This is the great tribute that the inhabitants of the cities, by practicing the highest ideals both in their way of living and in their discourse, have paid to the excellence of the Pharisees.

The Pharisees were a group in voluntary association with one another, who had particular views on Jewish religious life. For them not only the express commands of God set out in scripture were law, but also all rules that could be deduced from them in accordance with the accepted rules of legal reasoning. The rules so deduced are often called the "oral law."[27] They were not regarded by the Sadducees as authoritative. The Pharisees were to be found, above all, in Jerusalem. They were not the main priests, but were literate and very concerned with the law. When a Gospel text mentions "scribes," we may make a general presumption that this refers primarily to Pharisees. Their main concerns with law seem to have been ritual purity, food laws, and marriage. These are precisely the rules that a group under (foreign) domination can control for itself and even use to define itself, separate from the rest of society.

The Pharisees sought to keep themselves very much apart

from the rest of the people, and we find this recorded in several places in the Mishnah. Thus, Mishnah Hagigah 2.7 says that for the Pharisees the clothes of the 'am-ha'aretz, the people of the land, suffered the degree of uncleanliness known as *midras*. The 'am-ha'aretz were suspected of not paying tithes so that particular rules of Mishnah Demai ("Produce not certainly tithed") inhibited a *haver* (that is, a scrupulous observer of the law)[28] from buying from or selling to or otherwise dealing with them.[29] In particular, Mishnah Demai 2.3 declared that a haver "may not be a guest of an 'am-ha'aretz nor may he receive him as a guest in his own raiment." It is on account of their piety and intention to devote their lives to following in detail the laws of God that the Pharisees won the respect of other Jews.

In a very real sense the Pharisees were not a political party. Their concerns were religious, not secular. They wanted to fulfill the Torah rigorously. In so far as a government did not obstruct them in this, they could accept it. But by a seeming paradox, if a government appeared to oppose the performance of their religious practices or commit acts of hostility toward their religion, their enmity would be implacable, and they could seem to be intensely political.[30] At this stage it should be stressed that as people who saw themselves as a group apart they were not overly concerned with the less conscientious behavior of other Jews.[31] It would be wrong to regard them as engaging in conflict with Sadducees or the 'am-ha'aretz. In fact, such conflict does not appear in the Gospels.

The Gospels, moreover, make no distinction between one group of Pharisees and another, though the teachings of the one great school of Shammai were much more rigid than the teachings of the other great school of Hillel. Both these outstanding teachers lived from around the middle of the 1st century B.C. until well into the 1st century A.D. The Pharisaic views opposed to Jesus and those that he opposed are closer to the school of Shammai than to that of Hillel.

Josephus also described the Sadducees:

> *Jewish Antiquities* 18.16. The Sadducees hold that the soul perishes along with the body. They own no observance of any sort apart from the laws; in fact, they reckon it a virtue to dispute with the teachers of the path of wisdom that they pursue. 17. There are but few men to whom this doctrine has been made known, but these are men of the highest standing. They accomplish practically nothing, however. For whenever they assume some office, though they submit unwillingly and perforce, yet submit they do to the formulas of the Pharisees, since otherwise the masses would not tolerate them.

The Sadducees, we are told, accepted as binding only the law set out in Scripture, not also supplementary rules that could be deduced from it.[32] The Sadducees were the aristocratic members of Jewish society, and they filled the important priesthoods. The main priests were a closed group, and they had an exclusive right to sacrifice. They were the male descendants of Aaron, and none of those whose birth was accepted as legitimate could be excluded. Certainly, particular bodily defects would prevent them from sacrificing but would not exclude them from the group or from having their share in Temple taxes, sacrifices, and gifts. No observing Jew could do without them, and this gave them a respected position even if, as Josephus emphasizes perhaps with exaggeration, they accomplished little. For ordinary Jews, the Pharisees were the spiritual teachers and the Sadducees were the religious hereditary aristocrats whose lineage and formal role in society, but not their way of life, demanded respect. Their unshakable position before the Jews, their hereditary role in life, their wealth, and their prominence in society made them as a group more vulnerable to outside aggressors and, inevitably perhaps, more willing to collaborate with the Romans than were the Pharisees.[33]

Jesus was from Galilee, he was not a Sadducee, and, as we will see, he was hostile to Pharisaism. The Pharisees tended to regard the Galileans with some contempt as unlearned.[34]

A word should be said about the Mishnah, which has already been mentioned. This is a compendium of the early third century A.D., containing the rules, primarily legal rules, and arguments for the rules that are the basis of rabbinic judaism. The materials are drawn from scholars who flourished from around 50 B.C. to A.D. 200. Consequently, the information in it must not be accepted uncritically as recording stances held or accepted in the lifetime of Jesus. Moreover, at times one may suspect that the legal system portrayed was an ideal rather than a reality that had ever existed. Still, it does contain valuable information and insights for present purposes. Thus, rulings that were obsolete at the time of the compilation are often retained. The most obvious examples are the texts on sacrifices, although the Temple in Jerusalem—the only place where sacrifices could lawfully be made—had been destroyed by the Romans in A.D. 70. When appropriate for this book, I will discuss in subsequent chapters the reliance we may place on specific passages for the lifetime of Jesus.

It remains to mention in this brief historical survey that in the hellenistic world the belief in magic, in the efficacy of spells for good or evil, was extremely common and was found everywhere.[35] Miracle workers and magicians were often regarded as having particular connections with a deity or devil, or it was thought that the deity or devil worked through them. One example may stand for all. Vespasian, under whom the Temple was destroyed in A.D. 70, was in Alexandria in 69. He had just become emperor:

> Suetonius, *Divus Vespasianus* 7.2. He as yet lacked prestige and something akin to divine qualities because he was a new and unexpected emperor. But these were given to him. A man of the people who was blind and another who was lame together approached him as he was sitting on the tribunal begging for the help with their health which Serapis had promised in a dream. The god declared Vespasian would re-store the eyes if he spat in them; and would strengthen the leg if he would deign to touch it with his heel. 3. Though he had scarcely any faith that this would succeed in any way and therefore did not dare to make the attempt, he did try both things at the end because of the exhortation of his friends, before a very large crowd. And he had success.

The same miracles (with slight variations) are recorded by Taci-tus and Cassius Dio, and all three report other miracles in the time of Vespasian.[36] Thus, the emperor who destroyed the Jew-ish nation publicly performed miracles similar to Jesus' greatest. And in this he was not alone.

2

✠

ARREST,
TRIAL,
EXECUTION:
MARK

✠ ✠ ✠

AT THIS STAGE OF THE INVESTIGATION I HAVE TWO very limited aims. First, I wish to set out Jesus' interaction with others that could have led to his arrest and the consequences of that. Accordingly, Jesus' private words with his disciples are among the matters generally excluded. Second, I wish to set out the events in Mark to see whether the account is both internally consistent and internally plausible. That is, I do not want even to express an opinion on whether the events recounted give a plausible picture once external evidence is taken into account.

In Mark, Jesus' first brush with authorities, at the beginning of chapter 2, is with men designated as scribes. Jesus was teaching in a house at Capernaum to such a crowd that there was no room inside nor even outside around the door (2.2). Four men carried a paralyzed man, and when they could not bring him to Jesus they opened the roof and let down the mat on which the paralytic lay (2.3ff.). Seeing their faith, Jesus said to the paralytic, "Child, your sins are forgiven you" (2.5). Scribes who were present thought, "Why does he speak thus? He blasphemes. Who can forgive sins but God alone?" (2.7). Jesus understood what they were thinking, and said, "Why do you reason these things in your heart? What is easier, to say to the paralytic, 'Your sins are forgiven,' or to say, 'Rise, take your mattress, and walk'?" (2.9). "So that you [plural] should know that the son of man has authority to forgive sins on earth," he said, "To you [singular] I say, rise, take your mattress, and go to your house" (2.10f.). The paralytic took up his bed and walked. All were amazed and glorified God and said, "We have never seen anything like this" (2.12).

Jesus thus tells the paralytic, "Your sins are forgiven," but at first he does not heal him. Jesus is not alone in, at least at times, linking illness with sin.[1] The scribes do not confront him, though in their hearts they think he is a blasphemer.[2] "He blasphemes," βλασφημεῖ, is what the text records. They do not express their thoughts, so there is no attempt to entrap Jesus. Since these are reported to be their unspoken thoughts, they are to be treated as views honestly held. Certainly, Jesus' words do not technically constitute blasphemy as the crime is described in the later Mishnah and Talmud,[3] but no ordinary mortal can claim that someone's sin is forgiven: such a claim either usurps the authority of God or implies that the speaker knows the intention of God.[4] The words must inevitably be offensive. And Jesus has so far done nothing—nothing—to justify his words. Jesus reads the minds of the scribes and takes the initiative. He asks whether it is easier to say, "Your sins are forgiven" or "Take up your bed and walk." With this he seems to suggest that what he is being silently criticized for is his choice of words. But then he does claim he has authority to forgive sin, and he makes good his claim by performing the miracle. We are not given the reaction of the scribes unless they are included in all those who were amazed and glorified God. (But they might well have thought that in any event there was a distinction between a "holy" act, forgiveness, and a "magic" act, curing the paralytic.)

The remainder of Mark 2 is very busy, filled with three separate, apparently quite unconnected episodes: Jesus reclines in Levi's house at dinner with tax collectors and sinners (2.15ff.); Jesus is asked why his disciples do not fast as do those of John the Baptist and the Pharisees (2.18ff.); Jesus is asked why his disciples break the Sabbath by plucking grain (2.23). What elements are common to these episodes? First, none involves a miracle. Second, in two out of the three attention is focused on the behavior of the disciples, not that of Jesus himself. Third, only one, the last, could be portrayed as a significant breach of rabbinic law. Fourth, they are all relatively trivial. Fifth, they are all observed by the Pharisees: they see him reclining at dinner in the house of Levi, they notice his disciples do not fast, they follow him through the fields (plural) of grain on the Sabbath—at first sight also a breach of the Sabbath—and see that his disciples pluck grain. In none of the episodes are we given the Pharisees' reaction to Jesus' response. An explanation of these episodes is needed. I would suggest that after the miracle of curing the paralytic, which was seen by scribes, the Pharisees were keeping Jesus under close observation. But why do they raise questions about behavior that in others would be common and scarcely worth notice? The Pharisees, who saw themselves as a group apart, did not chase after the 'am-ha'aretz. My suggestion is that the Pharisees were trying to determine whether in any sense Jesus was akin to them, whether they could make common cause, whether they could even co-opt him, or whether he was a fraud they would want to expose. Their answer was finally negative. Jesus, at the beginning of Mark 2, had performed a miracle in full view of the scribes—though the words he had used were objectionable (unless he were the Messiah)— yet his subsequent behavior had shown he was not at one with the Pharisees. Their conclusion is displayed at the beginning of chapter 3, when Jesus cured a withered hand on the Sabbath. "The Pharisees went out and immediately conspired with the Herodians against him, how to destroy him" (3.6). The contrast between the overreaction at the beginning of Mark 3 and the silence over Pharisaic reaction in Mark 2 cries out. As often, the adage "If you can't beat them, join them" is turned on its head: "If he is not one of us, destroy him."

Jesus reclined at dinner in the house of Levi with tax collectors and sinners (2.15ff.). There was nothing greatly significant in Jewish law against eating with sinners, but in view of the ritual character of a Jewish meal it was unseemly, and especially so in someone with claims to special authority. The word *sinners* in this context is usually taken to mean the 'am-ha'aretz, who were less scrupulous than the Pharisees in observing the dietary law.[5] Moreover, as we saw in the previous chapter, Mishnah Demai 2.3 declared that a scrupulous observer of the law might not be a guest of an 'am-ha'aretz. Reclining rather than sitting even heightened the offense. It was usual for Jews to sit at meals, but reclining was obligatory at Passover and common for festive occasions.[6] So this meal with sinners was special. The Pharisees, it will be recalled, were stricter than other Jews in their observances.

Jesus was asked why his disciples did not fast when Pharisees and the disciples of John the Baptist fasted (2.18ff.). There were two kinds of fasts: general fasting, which was obligatory for everyone, and private fasting, which was voluntary.[7] The second kind is at issue here. In the last two centuries B.C. voluntary fasting had become an established custom within certain Jewish circles and was regarded as a sign of piety. Hence the interest in whether Jesus' disciples fasted and, presumably, the disquiet because they did not. The verse does not specify who posed the question: literally, "they come and they say," ἔρχονται καὶ λέγουσιν. There are three options. The Pharisees posed the question, the disciples of John the Baptist posed the question, or both groups did. Because of John's hostility to institutional religion we should exclude the possibility that the Pharisees and John's disciples posed the question together, and it seems superfluous to think two episodes have been condensed into one. In the context, because the episode is sandwiched between the first and third episodes in which John's disciples are not involved but Pharisees put the question, reason dictates that it was, indeed, the Pharisees who raised the issue.[8]

The Pharisees asked Jesus why his disciples plucked grain on the Sabbath, which they said was not lawful (2.23ff.). Plucking was regarded as reaping, which in the Mishnah is one of the forms of work forbidden on the Sabbath.[9] Jesus responds with a legalistic argument: there was a precedent. On another occasion, a Jewish leader in need (David, in fact) entered the house of God with his companions, and he ate the consecrated bread—which was not lawful—and gave some to his companions. As David Daube has shown, Jesus' argument is by no means conclusive.[10] The rabbis distinguished halakah, matters of law, from haggadah, matters of religious importance that did not affect the law. Any halakah had to rest directly or indirectly on Scripture. It need not be expressed in Scripture so long as it could be derived from Scripture by a recognized means of interpretation. Thus, the prohibition on plucking grain on the Sabbath was halakah: Scripture forbade working on the Sabbath, and by interpretation reaping was working. Historical data, on the other hand, could only amount to haggadah, which might inculcate moral lessons or wisdom but could never be a primary source of law. The example of David was thus haggadah. To the Pharisees, it would not be a convincing argument. In addition, David's behavior was not against the Sabbath, so in that way too it was not a good example for Jesus' argument. Further, what was regarded as permissible in a leader like David might not be permissible for lesser mortals. It may be noted in passing that Jesus scarcely uses legalistic arguments of any kind in John.[11]

In the episode at the beginning of Mark 3, the Pharisees were still tracking Jesus' behavior.[12] On the Sabbath he entered the synagogue where there was a man with a withered hand (3.1ff.). They watched to see whether Jesus would cure him so that they might accuse Jesus. Jesus asked the man to come forward (3.3), but at first he did not cure him. Instead he challenged the Pharisees: "Is it lawful to do good or do harm on the Sabbath, to save life or to kill?" (3.4). The Pharisees were silent, as well they might be. The question was unfair, and palpably so. There was no rabbinic prohibition on healing on the Sabbath, but on working. Healing might but need not involve working. Jesus became angry, and he healed the withered hand. Since we are not told how he effected the cure, we do not know whether it involved working or not. The Pharisees immediately conspired with the Herodians to destroy him (3.6). Their reaction was, of course, unjustified, but we should seek their reason. The reason cannot simply be that Jesus worked on the Sabbath. Rather, I suggest, Jesus, by confronting them and then proceeding to the cure, had shown his hostility to the Pharisees. He most definitely was not one of them and could not be co-opted. Jesus had consistently disregarded the Pharisees' understanding of religious law. The Herodians in the verse were presumably supporters of Herod Antipas, tetrarch of Galilee. The Pharisees would welcome the

Herodians' support because they could then more easily reach Jesus even in his own home area of Galilee, and at this time Jesus was in Galilee (2.1; 3.7). There is even an indication in 3.23 that the Pharisees had come from Jerusalem, so they would welcome local support. Why the Herodians would support the Pharisees is not clear.[13]

A feature of Mark that seems to be often overlooked is the very tight construction of the narrative.[14] Though the breaking into chapters is not original, we should note at this point that the four episodes in chapter 2 and the first in chapter 3 form a unit, with the last episode also serving as a transition. Thus, at the beginning of chapter 2 Jesus verbally confronts the scribes and then miraculously cures the paralytic. The Pharisees then follow Jesus and his disciples around, not to entrap him but to understand him and to see how his behavior corresponds to theirs. At the beginning of chapter 3 the Pharisees are still watching, but his confrontation with them on the Sabbath is the final proof that he is hostile, and this provokes them to enmity. Mark 3.23 continues this new theme of Pharisaic enmity.

Mark 1:40–45, the curing of the leper, also fits within this larger pattern, though the episode occurs before any confrontation with the Pharisees. Jesus is indignant at being asked to perform a miracle, but he does it and sends the cured man to a priest to receive ritual cleansing. The requirements for cleansing by a priest were laid down in Scripture.[15] This aspect of the pattern is miraculous cure with a regard for Scripture (1.40ff.); miraculous cure with a disregard for Pharisaic teaching and deliberate confrontation with Pharisees (2.2ff.); disregard for Pharisaic teaching (2.14ff.); recognition of divine law but disregard for Pharisaic interpretation (2.23ff.); miraculous cure with deliberate confrontation with Pharisees (3.1ff.); and Pharisaic anger (3.6).

(Scholars often feel that the disputes about Sabbath, purity, and food are probably not authentic. Even if some of the sayings are original, the settings, it is claimed, are contrived.[16] Pharisees would not follow Jesus through fields or go specially from Jerusalem to Galilee to check on whether the disciples washed their hands. This argument fails, I believe, if we postulate that the Pharisees developed an intense interest in Jesus when he cured the paralytic after his strange statement, "Child, your sins are forgiven you." Of course, they would want to know what kind of man he was and how his behavior related to them. Even how Jesus' disciples behaved would fascinate the Pharisees, for that would illumine his being.)

At 3.23 the scribes who had come from Jerusalem—more evidence that Jesus' actions were being watched—claimed, "He has Beelzebul, and by the ruler of the demons he casts out demons." Jesus' ability to perform miracles (3.11–15) was noted, but those hostile to him attributed this power to the devil. Miracle workers, it should be observed again, were common at that time. A subtext is that his family thought he had gone mad.[17] His family sought to seize him because he was out of his mind (3.21). The crowd told Jesus that his mother, brothers, and sisters were seeking him (3.32). He replied, "Who is my mother and my brothers?" (3.33). And he gave his own answer: "Whoever does the will of God, this one is my brother and sister and mother" (3.34). The point of all this is that in rabbinic law a lunatic was to be placed under the guardianship of his family, and Jesus' family wanted to place him under such restraint. Jesus' neat response was to deny that his natural family had any authority over him: those who had were those who did the will of God. The crowd was apparently sympathetic to Jesus' family, so the scribes' charge had some plausibility.

Still in Galilee, in his hometown of Nazareth he taught in the synagogue on a Sabbath (6.1). Many were astounded—on the one hand by his power, on the other because they knew him and his family—and they were offended by him. Jesus could do no deed of power there, apart from curing a few sick people. He was amazed at their unbelief (6.6). Thus, he had not won acceptance of his authority.

Herod Antipas, tetrarch of Galilee, heard of what Jesus and his disciples were doing (6.14)—a significant point because some were saying that Jesus was John the Baptist risen from the dead (6.14). Herod had had John arrested (6.17) and had been responsible for his execution (6.17ff.). Jesus took his disciples away to a deserted place (6.31ff.) but apparently still in Galilee. Many followed him, and he performed miracles.

Again, the narrative episodes that concern us—those leading up to Jesus' arrest—in chapters 3 through 6 form a tight unit. The constant theme is that Jesus performs miracles but is not accepted by the crowd or by his own family as someone with special spiritual authority. This pattern will continue: even his own disciples do not understand him.

Pharisees and some of the scribes who had come from Jerusalem asked Jesus why some of his disciples ate without the ritual hand washing (7.1ff.).[18] Jesus upbraided them as hypocrites. Then he mounted an attack on the oral law: "You abandon the commandment of God and hold to human tradition" (7.8).[19] In contrast to the Sadducees, the Pharisees, as we have seen, held as a group that the oral law—that derived by the appropriate, accepted modes of interpretation of the biblical laws—was binding (and was halakah). For example, God's prohibition in Scripture on working on the Sabbath gives no details. The very detailed rules in the Mishnah Shabbath are the result of interpretation and form the oral law. The rules so derived are synthesized into thirty-nine forms of prohibited work in Mishnah Shabbath 7.2.

In this context Jesus claims that the Mosaic laws "Honor your father and your mother" and "Whoever speaks evil of father or mother shall surely die" were set at naught by the Pharisaic interpretation that whatever support might have been given to parents by a son could be regarded as Corban, an offering to God (7.9ff.).[20]

As when disciples plucked ears of corn on the Sabbath, so here when disciples did not wash their hands before a meal, their behavior was not intended as a lesson. But in consequence of hostility to their behavior, Jesus used it to teach a lesson,[21] one that is aggressively critical of Pharisaic teaching. More than the disciples' behavior, Jesus' response must have provoked anger among the Pharisees.[22]

Some time later after he had gone to Tyre, Jesus returned to Galilee and performed miracles. Pharisees came to him, argued with him, and asked for a sign from heaven (8.11). He replied that no sign would be given to that generation (8.12). What the Pharisees were requesting was not a miracle of the kind that Jesus had been performing but some specific indication that his authority came from God. Given that miracle workers were not uncommon and that Jesus' teaching was contrary to that of the Pharisees, their request was not surprising—nor was their hostility.

At least part of what is going on is readily apparent. We are face to face with an ancient, well-known conflict: that between institutional authority and charismatic authority. College professors demand that new colleagues have doctoral degrees; a candidate with less formal training but with publications showing brilliant insights will be disregarded. Conventional, reputable scholars with weighty volumes setting out the pros and cons of other scholars' work will dismiss a book that plots a course of new thinking based on primary evidence but that is short on footnotes to secondary sources (including their own volumes). The Pharisees were the institutional religious authorities, and they knew Jesus threatened their status. But in this case, as in some others, the very deliberate instigator of the confrontation was the charismatic authority. He did not simply act and consequently face the hostility of the threatened institutional authority. Rather, he verbally challenged the institutional authority before publicly displaying his charismatic powers.[23]

Considerably later Jesus passed through Galilee. He did not want anyone to know it (9.30f.); on three separate occasions he told his disciples he would be put to death (8.31; 9.30f.; 10.32f.). The most specific prediction was the third:

> 10.32. He took the twelve aside again and began to tell them what was to happen to him, 33. saying, "See, we are going up to Jerusalem, and the Son of Man will be handed over to the chief priests and the scribes, and they will condemn him to death; then they will hand him over to the Gentiles; they will mock him, and spit upon him, and flog him, and kill him; and after three days he will rise again.

For our purpose this prophesy is central. It is unambiguous. Jesus will be handed over to the chief priests and the scribes, and they will condemn him to death. That is to say, he will be tried by the Sanhedrin, which will sentence him to death. The role reserved for the Roman occupying force is to carry out the execution. The importance of the prophesy is not as prophesy but as evidence of what, after the event, Mark thought had happened. The other two passages are less specific. They do not say who will put Jesus to death.

It is to be noted that up to this point at least, as set out by Mark, Jesus had said and done nothing that was inimical to the Romans. Nor had there been any indication of Roman hostility to Jesus. In contrast, Jesus' teachings were usually hostile to Pharisaic teachings, and some of his behavior and that of his disciples was contrary to Pharisaic tradition. The Pharisees had been following his movements and watching him, had shown hostility, and had even, we have been told, conspired with the Herodians to kill him. There had also been indications that Herod might seek to arrest him. Again, this is the first point in Mark which indicates that the chief priests were or would be involved: the indication is only in the prophesy, what will occur. Whereas the scribes were mainly Pharisees, the chief priests were Sadducees. Jesus by his words and actions had not shown himself to be hostile to the Sadducees, and there is no indication that the Sadducees followed Jesus to watch what he was doing or to seek to entrap him. They had no interest in him.

On the way to Jerusalem he had a triumphant reception (11.8ff.). Many spread their cloaks or leafy branches on the road before him. Both those in front of him and those behind him shouted, "Hosanna! Blessed is the one that comes in the name of the lord. Blessed is the coming kingdom of our father, David. Hosanna in the highest places" (11.9f.).

The precise meaning of the acclamation is unclear. *Hosanna* is usually regarded as a transliteration of the Aramaic word whose Hebrew equivalent is in Psalm 118.25. Literally, it means "help now" or "save now." In that sense it is used in addressing kings at 2 Samuel 14.4 and 2 Kings 14.4. But Psalms 113–18 were used together liturgically in synagogues on joyous festivals, and in this connection these Psalms were designated "Hallel." In this context the word *hosanna* would be known to everyone, but would be used as an acclamation of joy, even to a famous rabbi or pilgrim.[24] In its entirety Psalm 118 is a thanksgiving to God for deliverance in battle. Mark's "Blessed is the one that comes in the name of the lord" is an exact translation of part of Psalm

118.26, which continues, "We bless you from the house of the Lord." It is therefore a salutation or blessing to a pilgrim or rabbi who comes from outside and is uttered by those already in place. It is as a teacher or leader from afar that Jesus is welcomed by those of that place. In view of the Psalm's use at joyous festivals in general, it is doubtful whether its original nature as thanksgiving for delivery in battle should be stressed. The cry that follows in Mark, "Blessed is the coming kingdom of our father, David," is of obscure meaning. Mark does not trace Jesus' lineage; it is those who utter the cry who call David their father, and David is otherwise called "our father" only in Acts 4.25, where the precise intent is ambiguous. Besides, Bar Berakh 166 says that the term *fathers* was used only of Abraham, Isaac, and Jacob.[25] Jesus' response to the notion of a king descended from David is set out chapter twelve of this book.[26]

The acclamation was joyous and overwhelming: at last Jesus had the acceptance of the crowd. But though its precise meaning—if it had one—was unclear, there was nothing clearly expressed in it to show that the crowd actually believed Jesus was the Messiah.[27] In so far as that was true, there was nothing particular in the acclamation to trouble the Romans.

The next day Jesus came to Jerusalem:

11.15. And he entered the temple and began to drive out those who were selling and those who were buying in the temple, and he overturned the tables of the money changers and the seats of those who sold doves; 16. and he would not allow anyone to carry anything through the temple. 17. He was teaching and saying, "Is it not written,

'My house shall be called a house of prayer for all the nations?'
But you have made it a den of robbers."

18. And when the chief priests and the scribes heard it, they kept looking for a way to kill him; for they were afraid of him, because the whole crowd was spellbound by his teaching. 19. And when evening came, Jesus and his disciples went out of the city.

In effect, Jesus drove out of the Temple those who were buying and selling animals for the Passover sacrifice (although that they were selling animals for sacrifice is not made express). He overturned the tables of those who changed pagan didrachms and denarii into shekels so that the pilgrims could pay the Temple tax, and he overturned the seats of those who sold doves, which were the appropriate sacrifice of the poor. The presence of the cattle sellers was lawful in the Temple precincts,[28] the presence of the money changers was expressly permitted and regulated by rabbinic law,[29] and the sale of doves in the Temple for sacrifice was controlled by the Temple authorities.[30] Jesus' behavior was outrageous and deeply offensive to the Pharisees, to the Sadducees who had control of the Temple, and to observing Jews in general. Jesus had caused an uproar and assaulted individuals who performed services for the Temple. He had inhibited both the Passover sacrifices and the collection of the Temple dues. It can be no surprise that now the chief priests wanted to kill him—as we are told for the first time. In contrast to John, where nothing is said about the crowd's reaction, here the crowd was spellbound.

Jesus and his disciples left Jerusalem, then returned (11.27). The chief priests, scribes, and elders came to him when he was walking in the Temple, and they asked him, "By what authority are you doing [present tense] these things? or who gave you authority that you may do [present tense] these things?" (11.28). Whether "these things" were Jesus' acts in general or the so-called cleansing of the Temple is not clear, but the interest of the chief priests was specifically in the latter.[31] The use of the present tense is suggestive. Though the interrogators had in mind acts done in the past, the tense indicates concern for what Jesus would do next. They did not expect him to stop. Jesus' response was that he would ask one question. If they answered his question, he would answer theirs (11.29ff.). His question, whether the baptism of John was from God or men, presented them with a dilemma. They said they did not know the answer, and Jesus declared he would not tell them the authority by which he was doing (present tense in the Greek) these things.[32] In their eyes he thus compounded his outrageous behavior by refusing to explain or justify it. Jesus was again being confrontational. He was attempting to force his questioners to state publicly their stance on the problematic issue—better left undisturbed—of the authority of John the Baptist. If their reply was that John's authority was from men they would anger those who believed John was a prophet. If they answered, "From God," then they would be confirming the status of Jesus, whose greatness John had proclaimed.[33] Jesus then told a parable against the questioners (12.1ff.). When they realized its point, they wanted to arrest him, but they were afraid of the crowd (12.12).

The chief priests, scribes, and elders then sent some Pharisees and some Herodians to trap him by what he said (12.12). They led up to the question with skillful flattery: he is, they said, sincere, shows deference to none, but teaches the way of God in accordance with truth (12.13f.). They were paving the way for a straight answer. Then the question: "Is it lawful to pay taxes to the emperor, or not? Should we pay them, or should we not?" (12.14f.). (The Roman tax, it should be noted, is quite distinct from the Temple tax.) That we are told expressly that Herodians were involved is further evidence of what in any event is emphasized, namely, that this was a trick question. The Herodians were from Galilee, which was not a Roman province, hence they did not pay the Roman tax. The question had no practical relevance for them. To answer yes or to answer no was equally dangerous for Jesus. From the beginning of the Roman occupation the obligation to pay taxes had been a source of deep trouble. If Jesus said it was lawful to pay the tax, he would lose a great deal of popular support. It would be concluded he was not the Messiah, since one quality of the Messiah—and the Messiah was defined by particular qualities—was precisely that he would free Israel from foreign rule and make it the kingdom of God. If he said it was not lawful to pay the tax, he would seem to be inciting rebellion against the Romans, and he would be in trouble with the occupying power. Jesus' response was indirect (12.15). He asked for a denarius, pointed out that it portrayed the emperor, and said: "Give to the emperor the things that are the emperor's, and to God the things that are God's." The answer was subtle. On the face of it, it did amount to saying that it was lawful to pay the Roman tax; Jesus was avoiding conflict with the Romans. On the other hand, it drew a distinction between what is God's and what is not. There was more here than distinguishing two spheres of influence. It was obligatory to pay the other, the Temple tax, a tax in a sense to God. But it was not proper to pay that tax with denarii. The obverse of the denarius bore the bust of the emperor—a graven image. The reverse portrayed Livia, the emperor's mother, as the goddess Pax—even worse. Pious Jews should not want contact with denarii—denarii should go to the emperor. But Jesus' reply might be seen to have a hidden meaning. All things, it might be claimed, belonged to God.[34]

The posing of the question has another implication. It is a trick question: any straight answer will hurt Jesus with one group or another. This is a subject that should not be discussed publicly. But trick questions have limitations. This one could not be put if Jesus knew the answer that the Pharisees considered correct unless the Pharisees believed he would nonetheless give the opposite response. Thus, if the Pharisees considered paying the Roman tax to be lawful, they would put the question only if they thought Jesus would declare it unlawful. But Jesus has not shown himself to be hostile to the Roman occupation. He has no secular politics. If the Pharisees thought paying the tax to be unlawful, they would put the question only if they believed he would declare it lawful and thus make himself unpopular with the many who, we may presume, opposed secular taxes. A third possibility is that Pharisaic opinion was divided, and so Jesus would not know the answer the Pharisees wanted. The first possibility can, I suggest, be excluded. If this is so, then the fact that the Pharisees put the question indicates openly their hostility to Roman rule.

The Sadducees—naturally enough after the outrage in the Temple—were now also into the act of testing Jesus (12.18ff.). To their question about marriage law—at the Resurrection whose wife would a woman be who had married seven brothers in succession?—Jesus said they were wrong because they knew neither Scripture nor the power of God (12.24). Hostile as Jesus was to the Pharisees, he was also now having no truck with the Sadducees. But their question was not particularly hostile: it could not matter much to them whether Jesus believed in bodily resurrection and agreed with them in doctrine. The question was contemptuous.[35]

Jesus, teaching in the Temple, also warned the crowd to beware of the scribes (12.38ff.). Two days before the feast of the Passover, the chief priests and the scribes looked for a way to arrest Jesus by stealth and to kill him (14.1f.). They said, "Not during the festival, lest there be an uproar among the people"

(14.2). Judas Iscariot went to the chief priests to betray Jesus to them (14.10). This pleased them, and they promised to give him money (14.11). Judas looked for the opportunity.

After their Passover dinner, Jesus and his disciples went to a place called Gethsemane (14.32). Judas arrived with a crowd armed with swords and clubs, from the chief priests, the scribes, and the elders, and they arrested Jesus (14.43). This was not a rabble.[36] There was also no sign that Roman soldiers were involved. One of those standing by drew his sword and cut off the ear of the high priest's slave (14.47). That individual is not specifically identified as one of Jesus' disciples. Jesus complained that they had come with swords and clubs to arrest him as if he were a bandit, and that he had been with them, teaching in the Temple, and they had not arrested him (14.48f.). Jesus' disciples deserted him and fled (14.50). The crowd seems to have made little or no determined attempt to arrest the disciples, though one young man who was following him was seized, but he escaped leaving his one piece of clothing behind (14.50ff.).[37]

Jesus was taken to the high priest, and all the chief priests, elders, and scribes were assembled (14.53).[38] Two verses later we are told that the chief priests and the whole council were looking for testimony to put Jesus to death (14.55). These two verses indubitably point to a formal meeting of the Sanhedrin, the highest assembly or court of the Jews. Indeed, the word used in 14.55 for council is συνέδριον. As we shall see later, any such meeting would have been illegal. The Sanhedrin probably could not meet in a private house;[39] certainly it could not meet at night in a capital case.[40] Many gave false testimony against Jesus, and their testimony did not agree (14.56). The only false accusation against him that is spelled out is that he said he would destroy the Temple and within three days build another that was not made by hands (14.57f.). Even here their testimony did not agree (14.58). As we shall see in a subsequent chapter, requirements of proof before the Sanhedrin were very strict. The clear meaning of what Mark says is that the court did not have the evidence to convict Jesus. But why, it must be asked, if the judges were going to insist on keeping to the strict requirements of proof, did the Sanhedrin act so precipitously and illegally by holding the trial at night? The answer is that the chief priests and Pharisees had been desperate to arrest Jesus and finish the whole business ever since the cleansing of the Temple but were afraid to act during Passover because of the crowd.

The high priest intervened and asked Jesus for his response (14.60). Jesus made none (14.61).[41] The high priest asked if Jesus were the Messiah, and he replied that he was (14.61f.). The high priest then tore his clothes and asked why witnesses would still be needed when they had heard his blasphemy, and he asked for their decision. All condemned Jesus as deserving death (14.63–65). These three verses are particularly significant. They indicate that up to this point the evidence against Jesus was insufficient. But the high priest took the initiative and continued with the claim that Jesus' admission that he was the Messiah was blasphemous. Jesus' statement, as we shall see in chapter 8, probably was technically blasphemy at that time.[42] The high priest continued his initiative and tore his clothes. The point here is that the members of the council were obliged to rend their garments when someone was being found guilty of blasphemy. This is a sign of mourning. It is sometimes suggested that the high priest's action is not significant with regard to a verdict because Jews tore their clothes at other times of mourning. This interpretation is impossible. In a trial in which the high priest declared the accused to be blasphemous, the only possible symbolism of his tearing his clothes is condemnation of the accused. But then, it has been argued, all the judges should have torn their garments, not only the high priest. And he has done so at the wrong time, before condemnation to death at the second, morning session, which is the point of time specified in Mishnah Sanhedrin 7.5. Just so. The drama of Mark's account has been missed. The scenario is this. Although the meeting of the Sanhedrin was illegal, the judges insisted on observing the proper standards of evidence. On this basis, they could not reach a conviction. The high priest took matters into his own hands. He claimed that Jesus' admission in front of the council that he was the Messiah was blasphemy, asked what was the point of hearing other witnesses, and tore his clothes. He was acting as if Jesus were condemned to death! And the Sanhedrin acquiesced in his conduct and decided Jesus was worthy of death. High-handed bullying by the boss paid off, as it so often does. The underlings had the choice: face up to the hard-nosed chief and cause a confrontation, or go along. That in itself is always a difficult choice, and in this case the chief priests had no reason to be enthusiastic about Jesus anyway.

But there is much more to the issue of the high priest's high-handedness. The high priest was forbidden to rend his garments, not as a result of interpretation of Scripture but by Scripture itself. Leviticus 21.10 reads: "The priest who is exalted above his fellows, on whose head the anointing oil has been poured and who has been consecrated to wear the vestments, shall not dishevel his hair, nor tear his vestments."[43] The high priest's behavior is outrageous. He engages in a show of grief that is forbidden him but that is obligatory on his fellows. On this basis, only the most bitter and obdurate of the judges would refuse to follow him.

When it was morning, the chief priests held a consultation with the elders and scribes and the whole council (15.1). This is presumably in terms of the very important rule of Mishnah

Sanhedrin 5.5: "If they found him innocent, they set him free; otherwise they leave his sentence over until the morrow." The same rule stated that they should come together early in the morning. Mark does not tell us what sentence was decided upon, or even whether they decided upon a sentence at all. But they delivered Jesus, bound, to Pontius Pilate (15.1).

At this point I should like to pause again to show that there is no indication in Mark that Jesus was in any way an enemy of the Romans. Indeed, the evidence is all to the contrary.[44] In Mark, Roman soldiers were not involved in Jesus' arrest. No real attempt was made by the arresters to catch the disciples, which they would have done if the arresters had been soldiers and the disciples were the band of a revolutionary leader. Jesus' main hostility was directed against the Pharisees rather than the Sadducees, yet the latter were more openly collaborators with the Romans. In fact, the Pharisees were intent on preserving a particular Jewish way of life and separateness: this was at least part of the reason that the crowds admired them. Then, when directly asked, Jesus did not reply that it was illegal to pay tax to the Romans. Yet the supposed illegality of paying that tax appears to be the first ground of the Zealots' hatred of the Romans. Significantly, too, Jesus had a disciple called something like Simon the Zealot (3.18). This would be impossible if they were all Zealots. One would not call a Scot living in Scotland "David the Scot," but if David emigrated to the U.S.A. he might be thought of there as "David the Scot." Such appellations indicate a characteristic that separates the individual from his fellows.[45]

To return to the narrative, Jesus was delivered to Pilate. According to Mark, Pilate took the initiative and asked Jesus if he were king of the Jews (15.2). So Pilate must have had some prior knowledge of what was afoot. Of course he had. As we shall see in chapter 8, the procurator's consent was needed before the

Sanhedrin could meet. Jesus replied, "You say so." Basically this is no different from refusing to answer. The chief priests then accused him of many things (15.3). Mark does not state, however, that they told Pilate that they had tried him, or had found him guilty, or had condemned him to death. Pilate then wanted him to respond to what he termed the "many charges they bring against you" (15.4). The words indicate that for Mark the chief priests had not claimed to have convicted Jesus but had simply brought to Pilate accusations against him. Jesus made no answer to Pilate (15.5). The next few verses show that the immediate procedure had ended and that Pilate had made his decision.[46] Jesus, as we shall shortly see, was clearly treated as a prisoner who might be mercifully released, but in fact was crucified, and at that for sedition, treason against the Roman emperor.

But can it be claimed that there had been a proper Roman trial of a non-Roman before a provincial governor? The answer is a resounding yes, and we have the clearest possible evidence, though from a slightly later period.[47] Pliny the Younger was governor of Bythinia from around A.D. 100 to 102, and he wrote from there to the emperor Trajan for advice about the trials of persons who were supposed to be Christians:

In the meantime, I have followed this approach with regard to those who were denounced to me as Christians. I asked them whether they were Christians. I asked those who confessed a second time and a third time, having threatened torture. Those who still persevered I ordered to be executed. For I did not doubt, whatever their faith was, that their pertinacity and inflexible obstinacy deserved punishment.[48]

The offense considered by Pliny was to be a Christian; that charged against Jesus was the more serious offense of treason. Earlier in the letter Pliny had expressed uncertainty as to whether being a Christian was in itself the crime.[49] Now he is saying in effect that whether or not it was a crime, for an accused person to admit three times that he was a Christian was so objectionable in itself that he deserved to be, and would be, executed. To refuse to reply to the governor's, Pilate's, question was to show equal obstinacy. And Pliny, in contrast to Pilate, has the reputation for moderation and fair-mindedness.[50] Moreover, Jesus was not a Roman citizen, so Pilate had no need to respect the niceties reserved for them in a capital trial.

What is going on at this stage in Mark is clear beyond a shadow of a doubt. When the Sanhedrin met in the morning to give their official verdict, enough of the judges were ashamed of the illegality of the trial, of the failure of appropriate evidence, of their acceptance of the high priest's outrageous bullying, and of the wrong verdict of blasphemy, or they were afraid of the mob, that they refused to convict. No other scenario would explain why they did not put Jesus to death by stoning, but instead handed him over to Pilate, for whom blasphemy was no crime. The charge brought against Jesus by Pilate was treason to the Roman emperor, and he was properly tried and put to death. But in the final analysis he was not convicted of any capital offence by the Sanhedrin, and he was not executed by the Jews. In Mark, the failure of the Sanhedrin to convict is played down. (Indeed, the evangelist may not have been conscious of it.)

Pilate had a custom, Mark says, to release one prisoner to the Jews at Passover, whomever they wished (15.6). The crowd asked him to follow his custom and to release Barabbas, a captured brigand (15.7f.). Pilate offered instead "the king of the Jews," because he knew that the chief priests had delivered Jesus out of jealousy (15.9f.). But the chief priests stirred up the crowd to demand Barabbas (15.11). When Pilate asked what should be done with "the man you call the king of the Jews," they insisted upon crucifixion (15.12). Barabbas was released; Jesus was flogged (15.15), which was the normal preliminary to a crucifixion. Jesus was crucified at nine in the morning (15.25). The charge against him was inscribed "The King of the Jews" (15.26).

The whole account of the arrest, trial, and execution of Jesus, ending with a Roman provincial trial on the charge of a Roman crime, ending in a Roman execution, is internally consistent. Whether the account is historically plausible or accurate will be determined later.

3

✠

ARREST,
TRIAL,
EXECUTION:
JOHN

✠ ✠ ✠

JESUS' FIRST OPEN CLASH WITH AUTHORITY IN JOHN is the "cleansing of the Temple" (2.13ff.). This account differs from those in the Synoptics in two important ways. First, in the Synoptics it occurs at the end of Jesus' ministry and leads directly to his arrest. In John it is at the very beginning of Jesus' ministry. Second, in John it is recounted with much more detail. The specificity in John makes Jesus' behavior much more outrageous.[1]

In John we learn that the Temple merchants were selling cattle, sheep, and doves (2.14). In Mark we have only that Jesus drove out those who were buying and selling and that he overturned the tables of those selling doves. That the "sellers" in Mark are in John "sellers of cattle and sheep," not other unspecific sellers, makes Jesus' behavior very offensive. The sellers were there for the benefit of pilgrims who had come to sacrifice at Passover. Animals for sacrifice had to meet stringent requirements[2] and would not be easily found by those coming for the festival if it were not for the sellers in the Temple precincts. No prohibition against buying sacrificial animals in the Temple existed, and Mishnah Shekalim 7.2 shows incidentally that the presence there of the sellers was both lawful and known. The sale of doves for sacrifice in the Temple at any time was even controlled by Temple authorities.[3] Moreover, only in John did Jesus make a whip of cords, and he used it not only on the people but also on the sheep and cattle. In John Jesus was out of control. His behavior involved physical assault in the Temple precincts and obstructed the Passover sacrifices and the collection of Temple taxes. From the standpoint of rabbinic law, Jesus' behavior was incomprehensible and criminal. The "cleansing" was a direct attack on all observing Jews, Pharisees, and Sadducees alike. The Jews' reaction is not described.

Jesus was asked what sign he could give for his behavior (2.18). He replied, "Destroy this Temple, and in three days I will build it up." This reply was incomprehensible and, on its face, offensive. The reaction of the Jews is not stated.

Jesus learned that the Pharisees had heard that he was baptizing—he was not, but his disciples were—and he left Judaea to return to Galilee. But on the way he had to go through Samaria (4.1–4). Apparently he was in no rush to reach Galilee, for he delayed two days in Samaria (4.39–43). This is revealing. If Jesus had been fleeing from the Romans—which is not stated or implied—he would not have delayed in Samaria, because Samaria was part of the Roman province of Judaea, and he would be little safer there. On the other hand, Samaria was the territory of the Samaritans, and the Pharisees—whom Jesus was said to be avoiding—had even less power there than in Galilee.

Jesus healed the paralytic at the pool of Beth-zatha on a Sabbath (5.1ff.), but to effect the cure he caused the paralytic to break the Sabbath by carrying his mat. According to the rules set out in Mishnah Shabbath 7.2, this amounted to the exparalytic working. Therefore, the Jews started persecuting Jesus (5.16). Jesus then claimed God worked on the Sabbath in the same way that he did (5.17). But Jesus was being blamed for working in ways that were forbidden. For him now to claim in response that God so worked on the Sabbath was to deny the Sabbath. And Judaism without the Sabbath was unthinkable. It is no surprise that we are then told that "all the more" did the Jews seek to kill him.[4]

Jesus fed a multitude, who then followed him across the Sea of Galilee (6.1–13). Jesus told them that they followed him because they had eaten their fill of bread (6.26). He said his Father gave them bread from heaven (6.32ff.). They asked for it (6.34), and Jesus said, "I am the bread of life" (6.35). The Jews complained on this account (6.41), and Jesus told them he was the living bread from heaven and that unless they ate his flesh and drank his blood they would have no life in them (6.51–58). Because of this teaching, even many of his disciples left him (6.66). Indeed, the words would horrify believing Jews. At the very least they are a command to cannibalism. And human flesh is forbidden meat. After this, Jesus went about in Galilee but not in Judaea because the Jews were seeking to kill him (7.1). Nonetheless, he did return to Jerusalem in secret (7.10) and taught in the Temple. He accused the people of trying to kill him, and they denied it (7.19ff.). Some Jerusalemites asked themselves if he was the man they were seeking to kill because there he was speaking openly, and they wondered if in fact the authorities really knew that he was the Messiah (7.25ff.). They tried to arrest him, but failed (7.30). When the Pharisees heard what the crowd was saying, they sent Temple police to arrest him, but likewise in vain (7.32ff.).

Jesus spoke to the Pharisees in a way offensive to them (8.12ff.). He said, "Before Abraham was, I am" (8.58), thus implying his divinity, and they picked up stones to throw at him (8.59). This was an attempt at lynching, and no crime by Jesus is specified.

Jesus restored the sight of one blind from birth on a Sabbath (9.1ff.). That man spoke back to the Pharisees when they questioned him, and they drove him out. Subsequently, Jesus said, "The Father and I are one" (10.30) and the Jews once more attempted to stone him (10.31). Again, this was attempted lynching. Their justification was that Jesus was guilty of blasphemy by claiming to be God (10.33). They tried to arrest him again (10.34), which shows the attempted stoning was extralegal. To this point, the only enemies of Jesus whom we are told about are the Pharisees.

Jesus returned to Judaea (11.7) and raised Lazarus from the dead (11.1ff.). Some who saw him told Pharisees (11.46), and they and the chief priests called a meeting of the Sanhedrin (11.47). There it was claimed that if the people believed in Jesus, the Romans would destroy both the holy place and the nation (11.48). The high priest, Caiaphas, who was a Sadducee (or he would not have been the high priest), declared it was expedient that one man die for the nation (11.50).

Jesus went to Ephraim (11.54) but returned to Bethany six days before the Passover (12.1). The chief priests planned to put Lazarus to death also (12.10).

After the Last Supper Jesus went across the Kidron Valley with his disciples (18.1). Judas brought a detachment of soldiers together with police from the chief priests and Pharisees, and they arrested Jesus (18.3ff.). The soldiers were led by an officer with the rank of military tribune. This is the first mention of Roman involvement. They took Jesus not to the Roman praetorium but to the house of Annas, who was Caiaphas's father-in-law (18.13) and a respected former high priest. This can be plausibly explained. Presumably Pilate, then as later, was reluctant to be involved in a matter that could lead to rioting, and in any event the chief priests wanted to examine Jesus. That the Romans were less than enthusiastic in the arrest is clear from the fact that they made no attempt to arrest the disciples. Annas sent Jesus, bound, to Caiaphas (18.24). Early in the morning they took Jesus to Pilate's headquarters (18.28). Nothing in the account indicates that Jesus was formally tried by the Sanhedrin, and the earlier meeting of which we are told, before the arrest, was a council session, not a trial. The Sanhedrin could not lawfully hold a capital trial at night or, probably, in a private house. Accordingly, for John we have no need to inquire into the crime Jesus was charged with before the Sanhedrin.

Pilate asked those who brought Jesus what charge they were bringing against him (18.29). They evasively replied that if Jesus were not a criminal they would not be handing him over to Pilate (18.30) and that they were not permitted to put anyone to death (18.32). This last statement, as we shall see in chapter 8, is incorrect. Pilate asked Jesus whether he was a king, and received no answer. This obduracy, no matter what the charge, would be enough to explain the sentence of flogging and crucifixion. An almost exact parallel, as we have seen, is in Pliny *Epistulae* 10.96. Still, in light of the questions put and of the inscription on the cross, Jesus was put to death for maiestas (high treason).

(In passing, we should nonetheless emphasize that in his book, *Roman Society and Roman Law in the New Testament*, A. N. Sherwin-White, citing Lietzman, is wildly inaccurate in his account of what John records. Sherwin-White says of the trial by Pilate: "in which the offence against the Jewish law is twice made the principal charge," he then has a footnote to John 18.30f. and 19.7, and he concludes that the Sanhedrin had condemned Jesus for blasphemy.[5] But in John 18.31, Pilate is made to say expressly, "Take him yourselves and judge him according to your law." Thus, the Sanhedrin had not already judged Jesus, far less condemned him. In John 19.7 we have: "The Jews answered him, 'We have a law, and according to that law he ought to die because he has claimed to be the Son of God.' " But nothing in that text suggests that the Sanhedrin had condemned Jesus.)

The account as we have it in John is internally consistent, even though it is so very different from that in Mark. Again, there is no sign that Jesus was an enemy of Rome or that he feared the Romans. When from anxiety about the Pharisees he left Judaea to return to Galilee (John 4.1ff.), he delayed two days in Samaria. This he would not have done if he had feared Roman intervention. Roman involvement occurs only at the point of Jesus' arrest, and it supports Caiaphas's assertion, after the raising of Lazarus, that if Jesus continued the Romans would destroy the Temple and the nation. This was reasonable: if Jesus could raise from the dead, what army might he not produce against the Romans? Still, the Roman authorities were not worried. They made no attempt to arrest the disciples as they would have done if they were regarded as revolutionaries, and they were quite content to have the main interrogation be conducted in the houses of Annas and Caiaphas. In John, Jesus is no Zealot or enemy of Rome.

From the earliest days of his ministry Jesus in John is extremely hostile to the external trappings of Judaism as evidenced in the Pharisees. The Temple is cleansed by a man out of control whose rage is not focused on one sect but on Pharisees, Sadducees, and all observing Jews alike. The reaction to this is not given, but afterwards Jesus is represented as having some fear of the Pharisees (4.1ff.).

Jesus continued his behavior, which must have seemed outrageous especially to the Pharisees, who had a strict understanding of the prohibition of working on the Sabbath (5.1ff.). The paralytic was forced to break the Sabbath if he wanted to be cured. Jesus went further and, in effect, denied the Sabbath. This would seem outrageous to any Jew, since without the Sabbath there can be no Judaism.

Subsequently, Jesus was verbally offensive to the Pharisees, and they wanted to lynch him. By now (10.30) Jesus' words were again intolerable to the Pharisees, and they again tried to lynch him. Later they attempted to arrest him (10.39). To this point, the only enemies of Jesus who are identified are Pharisees, and they have cause. But so have the Sadducees and all observing Jews, after the cleansing of the Temple. After the raising of Lazarus, Jesus could reasonably appear to be a danger to the Temple and the nation. A meeting of the Sanhedrin took place, and the Sadducean high priest, Caiaphas, took the not unreasonable position that it was expedient that one man die for the nation (11.50). This is not represented as anger in general against Jesus' behavior or beliefs.

Jesus was arrested by a detachment of Roman soldiers and police of the chief priests and Pharisees. Jesus was taken to the house of Annas, not to the Roman prætorium. This is consistent with a Roman lack of concern. There was an interrogation there and in the house of Caiaphas, but no trial before the Sanhedrin. Jesus was delivered to Pilate, who tried him briefly and without enthusiasm and executed him for treason.

Thus, Jesus was no enemy of Rome but was outstandingly hostile to Jewish observances. Still, despite his wild behavior, reaction to him at first was muted. Subsequent behavior, even to the extent of denying the Sabbath, outraged the Pharisees to the point that they sought to kill him. Still, only when he posed a real threat to the Temple and nation did the Sadducees also wish his death. The Jewish authorities involved the Romans in the arrest. The first interrogations were by the Jewish authorities, but they avoided a trial before the Sanhedrin. They involved the Roman authorities further by charging Jesus with crimes. Under pressure Pilate tried him for treason, convicted, and executed him.

In *Jesus and the Jews: The Pharisaic Tradition in John*, I examined the narrative in episodes that occurred only in John and not in the Synoptics, or that occurred in John and the Synoptics but where John's version was significantly different from the others. My main conclusions there have little bearing on the arguments of this book, but since I touch on them in a few places, it is proper to set them out here to avoid confusion. John for me as for most other scholars is a composite work, with the evangelist making use of more than one existing tradition or source. I believe that the main narrative source for the episodes that appear only in John, or with significant differences in John, is an anti-Christian Pharisaic tradition, which for convenience I have designated S. In any community where there were numerous Jews shortly after the death of Jesus, where some believed Jesus was the Messiah and most did not, conflicting traditions inevitably would have developed, often using the same episodes but to different effect. One such Pharisaic tradition, I believe, was incorporated into S, perhaps in response to a tradition such as that in Mark. S showed Jesus as a miracle worker because his fame as such was too strong to be much contested. But for this tradition Jesus was not the Messiah, and it portrayed him as a rather unsavory individual, much given to outbursts of rage, who was very hostile to Jewish law and to the Pharisees, and much of whose behavior was geared toward insulting or injuring the Jews. A prime concern of S was to legitimize the role of Jewish leaders in the death of Jesus. The tradition of S was too well known for the evangelist John to ignore it. Instead, he incorporated parts of it into his writing, making small but significant changes to defang it and adding his theological message. But, as is standard with composite works, important traces of the sources shine through. It remains to add that the S tradition was fully informed of circumstances in Jerusalem before the destruction of the Temple. John the evangelist, on the other hand, had little understanding of Jewish circumstances and, as I suggested in the preface, the gaffes are his responsibility.

4

✠

MATTHEW
AND
LUKE

✠ ✠ ✠

AN EXAMINATION OF MATTHEW AND LUKE WILL, I
believe, eventually take us closer to historical plausibility, but
again we must first set out the course of events.

In Matthew, when John was baptizing, many Pharisees and
Sadducees came for baptism, and he abused them, calling them
a brood of vipers (3.7ff.). Hostility to these particular groups on
the part of John the Baptist is not recorded by Mark, Luke, or
John. When Jesus heard that John had been arrested, he withdrew, we are told, to Galilee (4.12). Thus, Jesus feared he would
be regarded as guilty by association. But something is not quite
right. John was arrested by Herod Antipas, tetrarch of Galilee, so
Galilee should be the last place anyone would go seeking refuge
from him.

The healing of the paralytic that we have already seen in Mark
recurs but with differences.

> 9.2 And they brought to him a paralytic who had been
> laid on a mattress, and Jesus, seeing their faith, said to

the paralytic: "Be of good cheer, child, your sins are forgiven." 3. And behold, some of the scribes said among
themselves: "This man blasphemes." And Jesus, knowing
their thoughts, said: "Why do you think evil things in your
heart? 5. For which is easier, to say, 'Your sins are forgiven,' or to say, 'Rise and walk'? 6. But so that you may
know that the Son of Man has authority on earth to forgive
sins," [he says to the paralytic] "Rise, take your mattress
and go home." 7. And he rose and took his mattress, and
went home. 8. The crowds, seeing this, feared and glorified
God who gave such authority to men.

In Mark, the thoughts of the scribes were not spoken. Jesus
took the initiative in questioning them. In Matthew the scribes
said among themselves that Jesus blasphemed. In the passage
from Matthew set out above, it becomes apparent that Matthew
has deviated from the original. In 9.3 the words "Jesus knowing
their thoughts" indicates that the scribes had not spoken them
aloud. The words are borrowed from Mark where they are appropriate. Much of the power of the version in Mark is lost.[1] In
general, Matthew appears to demystify Mark.

Three episodes were recounted in the rest of Mark 2. The
same three episodes recur in Matthew but again with significant
differences. Only two of the episodes are in Matthew 9 after
Jesus' healing of the paralytic. Jesus' dining with tax collectors
and sinners is told (9.10ff.) in much the same way as in Mark.
But those who ask why Jesus' disciples do not fast are here expressly disciples of John the Baptist (9.14ff.). Then only in the
rather distant context of 12.1ff. is Jesus asked by the Pharisees
why his disciples pluck grain on the Sabbath. The inference I
drew from the three episodes in Mark was that they should be
taken together to show that the Pharisees were following Jesus

to see if he could be co-opted or if he was a fraud. No such inference can be drawn in Matthew. The structure is much looser. Still, the four episodes so far examined are reported in Mark and Matthew in the same order.

Jesus cured the withered hand on a Sabbath, and the Pharisees conspired how to destroy him (12.9ff.). The episode is recounted much as in Mark, though in Matthew there are two differences. First, in Mark it was Jesus who confronted the Pharisees and escalated the problem. Here it is the Pharisees who started the confrontation. For me, the episode in Mark could be linked in a historical or storylike way with the three immediately preceding episodes. Here it cannot. The second difference is that in Mark there is no mention of the Herodians joining the Pharisees. Again the order of episodes is the same in Mark and Matthew.

At 12.24 after another miracle when crowds were wondering whether Jesus was the Son of David, the Pharisees said, "It is only by Beelzebul, the ruler of the demons, that this fellow casts out the demons." But there is no subtext in Matthew that Jesus' family wanted to treat him as a lunatic: we do not see in Matthew the same popular suspicion of Jesus. Matthew prefers an unproblematic Jesus.

Then some of the scribes and Pharisees asked for a sign (12.38). As in Mark 8.11, they meant not just a miracle but evidence that his authority came from God. As in Mark Jesus refused, but with more vehemence: "An evil and adulterous generation asks for a sign, but no sign will be given to it except the sign of the prophet Jonah" (12.39). Again in Matthew, at 16.1ff., both Pharisees and Sadducees asked for a sign from heaven and got a similar response. The interest of the Sadducees in Jesus is new, though both Sadducees and Pharisees had been abused by John the Baptist.

Herod Antipas came to believe that Jesus was John the Baptist raised from the dead (14.1ff.), so Jesus withdrew to a deserted place (14.13). Pharisees and scribes came from Jerusalem to seek him out (15.1ff.), and asked why his disciples did not wash their hands before eating. His response was very much as in Mark 7.1ff. Again, all the episodes are recounted in the same order in Matthew and Mark.

Later Jesus tells his disciples that he must go to Jerusalem and suffer many things from the elders, chief priests, and scribes and be killed (16.21). Who will kill him is not specified here but is in 20.18 when Jesus takes up the subject again. The chief priests and scribes will condemn him to death and hand him over to the Gentiles to be mocked, flogged, and crucified. Next comes the cleansing of the Temple (21.12ff.), which is reported in a very similar way to Mark. As in Mark, Jesus, while he was teaching, was asked by the chief priests and elders the authority by which he acted, and he replied in a similar manner (21.23ff.). He also told a parable against the chief priests and Pharisees, and they wanted to arrest him but were afraid of the crowd (21.46). Seeking to entrap him, the Pharisees with the Herodians asked the same question about paying tax to the Romans and received the same answer (22.15ff.).

After the Passover dinner Jesus went with his disciples to Gethsemane (26.36). Judas arrived with a large crowd carrying swords and clubs, sent by the chief priests and the elders (26.47), and they arrested Jesus (26.50). One of the disciples drew his sword and cut off the ear of the high priest (26.51). The disciples deserted and fled (26.56). No mention is made of any attempt to arrest them. Those who arrested Jesus took him to the house of Caiaphas, the high priest, where the scribes and elders were gathered (26.57). There was a meeting of the Sanhedrin ($\sigma \upsilon \nu \acute{\epsilon} \delta \rho \iota o \nu$) (26.59), and we are expressly told they were looking for false testimony in order to put Jesus to death, but they found none, although many false witnesses came forward (26.60).[2] Then two witnesses claimed they had heard Jesus say he was able to destroy the Temple of God and rebuild it in three days. The high priest asked Jesus for his response, but he gave none (26.63). The high priest asked if he were the Messiah,[3] took his answer—"You have said it"—as positive, then tore his clothes and said, "He has blasphemed! Why do we still need witnesses? You have now heard his blasphemy. What is your verdict?" (26.65f.). They answered, "He deserves death" (26.66). So Jesus was tried by the Sanhedrin and convicted.

In the morning, they all met again and discussed how to bring about Jesus' death. Then they bound him and handed him over to Pilate (27.1f.). Nothing is said about whether they again found him guilty and fixed his sentence. Only at this stage in Matthew do Romans become involved.

But Matthew now inserts an episode that was not in Mark and that, although not part of the events leading up to Jesus' arrest, the arrest itself, the trial and execution, is illuminating for Matthew's understanding:

27.3 When Judas, his betrayer, saw that Jesus was condemned, he repented and brought back the thirty pieces of silver to the chief priests and the elders. 4. He said, "I have sinned by betraying innocent blood." But they said, "What is that to us? See to it yourself." 5. Throwing down the pieces of silver in the temple, he departed; and he went and hanged himself. 6. But the chief priests, taking the pieces of silver, said, "It is not lawful to put them into the treasury, since they are blood money." 7. After conferring together, they used them to buy the potter's field as a place to bury foreigners. 8. For this reason that field has been called the Field of Blood to this day. 9. Then was fulfilled what had been spoken through the prophet Jeremiah. "And they took the thirty pieces of silver, the price of the one on whom a price had been set, on whom some of the people of Israel had set a price, 10. and they gave them for the potter's field, as the Lord commanded me."

Full of remorse, Judas admitted to the chief priests and elders that he had betrayed an innocent man. When the authorities refused to have anything to do with the matter, he hanged himself. The point of this is that under rabbinic law a bearer of false evidence should suffer the penalty appropriate to the supposed crime: death, in this case.[4] Judas is acting as if Jesus had been condemned. Indeed, 27.3 says, "Judas seeing . . . that he was condemned" ($κατεκρίθη$). So for Matthew the Sanhedrin had confirmed its verdict, though this emerges only in a very indirect way.[5]

But Jesus was now before Pilate, who asked if he were the king of the Jews, and Jesus replied, "You say so" (27.11). The chief priests and elders now accused him, and he answered nothing (27.12). Pilate asked if he had heard the many accusations, and again he did not respond (27.13f.). This amounts to a trial before the Roman governor, and the priests and elders brought only secular accusations against Jesus, not a religious trial verdict and sentence. There is thus confusion in Matthew.

As in Mark, the proceedings before Pilate are a trial, and Jesus was convicted. The trial was for the Roman secular crime of treason (27.37), and Jesus was crucified.

We come now to Luke. In Luke, many came to John the Baptist to be baptized, and he called them a "brood of vipers" (3.7). The makeup of the crowd is not described. Herod imprisoned John, because John rebuked him over marrying Herodias, his brother's wife (3.19). There is no indication of any effect of this on Jesus. Jesus taught in Galilee and was praised by everyone (4.15). He went to Nazareth where he had been brought up, and read from the scroll in the synagogue, interpreting it to refer to himself personally as one particularly favored by God (4.16ff.). All were amazed at his gracious words, but they asked, "Is this not Joseph's son?" (4.22f.). Jesus took offense and said, among other things, that no prophet is accepted in his home-town (4.23ff.). The people were enraged, drove him out of town, and wanted to throw him over a cliff, but Jesus escaped (4.29f.). Thus, Jesus' first conflict was with the people in a synagogue in Galilee, not specifically with Pharisees or Sadducees, and he brought it on by claiming to be an unrecognized prophet.

Jesus' fame spread as both teacher and miracle worker. One day when he was teaching, Pharisees and teachers of the law who had come from every village of Galilee and Judaea and from Jerusalem were sitting around (5.17). The paralytic was brought to Jesus, and because of the crowd, his friends lowered him through the roof (5.18ff.). Jesus said, "Man, your sins have been forgiven" (5.20). The Pharisees and scribes began to reason and said, "Who is this who speaks blasphemies? Who, except God, can forgive sins?" (5.21). Jesus knew their thoughts, and the episode continues as in Mark and Matthew. In Luke, as in Matthew but in contrast to Mark, it is the Pharisees, not Jesus, who began the confrontation by saying that Jesus was a blas-phemer. As in Matthew, Luke reveals that it proceeds on the original version that was in Mark: Jesus understood what they were thinking, not what he had heard, as appears from his words, "Why do you raise such questions in your hearts?" (5.23).

The three episodes then recounted in Mark, 2, next appear in Luke in exactly the same order as in Mark and Matthew (5.29–35; 6.1–5).[6] But this time, those who ask why his disciples do not fast are very clearly the Pharisees and scribes, not the disciples of John the Baptist as in Matthew, nor is the identity of the questioners left slightly ambiguous as in Mark. The episode of the disciples plucking heads of grain comes in Luke immediately after the question about the disciples fasting (6.1ff.). As in Mark the Pharisees were following Jesus to see what he said and did. Next, as in Mark and Matthew, comes the curing of the withered hand (6.6ff.). As in Mark, but contrary to Matthew, it is Jesus who takes the lead in the confrontation (6.8). The scribes and Pharisees are filled with madness and discuss what they might do to Jesus. Rather later on, we have Jesus declaiming:

> 7.31 "To what then will I compare the people of this generation, and what are they like? 32. They are like children sitting in the marketplace and calling to one another,
>
>> 'We played the flute for you, and you did not dance; we wailed, and you did not weep.'
>
> 33. For John the Baptist has come eating no bread and drinking no wine, and you say, 'He has a demon'; 34. the Son of Man has come eating and drinking, and you say, 'Look, a glutton and a drunkard, a friend of tax collectors and sinners!'"

The people he is referring to, as we know from the preceding verse 30, are Pharisees and scribes who refused to be baptized by John the Baptist. They must have said threatening things about Jesus because the accusation made against him refers to Deuteronomy 21.18–21, especially verse 20:

> 18. If someone has a stubborn and rebellious son who will not obey his father and mother, who does not heed them when they discipline him, 19. then his father and his mother shall take hold of him and bring him out to the

elders of his town at the gate of that place. 20. They shall say to the elders of his town, "This son of ours is stubborn and rebellious. He will not obey us. He is a glutton and a drunkard." 21. Then all the men of the town shall stone him to death. So you shall purge the evil from your midst; and all Israel will hear, and be afraid.

Since "drunkard and glutton" are part of the formula intoned by parents of a stubborn and rebellious son, we may have another indication, as we had in Mark, that Jesus' relatives were not convinced of his ministry. The penalty was death by stoning.[7] (In passing I should state that I doubt that this penalty was often, if ever, enforced. But that does not lessen the implicit menace of the accusation. So potent to the imagination is the nature of this offense that it appears again in § 14 of *The General Laws and Liberties concerning the Inhabitants of the Massachusetts of 1648*.)

In the house of a Pharisee, a sinful woman anointed Jesus' feet, and he told her that her sins were forgiven (7.48). Those at table with him said among themselves, "Who is this who even forgives sins?" (7.49).[8]

Herod heard of Jesus' miracles and wondered who he was: some said he was John raised from the dead (9.7ff.). Jesus withdrew with his disciples to Bethsaida (9.10).

He performed other miracles, but when he cast out a devil some said, "He casts out demons by Beelzebul, the ruler of the demons" (11.15). Who these people were is not stated. Others asked him for a sign from heaven (11.16). So, despite the miracles, many were unconvinced that his powers came from God. Later he told the increasing crowd that the present generation was an evil generation: it asked for a sign, he said, but no sign would be given except the sign of Jonah (11.29).

A Pharisee invited Jesus to dinner and was amazed that Jesus did not wash before dinner (11.37ff.). This leads into Jesus' violent diatribe against Pharisees and lawyers.[9] The scribes and Pharisees became very hostile and cross-examined him about many things, lying in wait to catch him out (11.53f.).

Jesus was teaching in the synagogue one Sabbath when he cured a crippled woman (13.10ff.). The leader of the synagogue was angry and said that the sick should come to be cured on the other six days, not on the Sabbath (13.14).

> 15. But the Lord answered him and said, "You hypocrites! Does not each of you on the sabbath untie his ox or his donkey from the manger, and lead it away to give it water? 16. And ought not this woman, a daughter of Abraham whom Satan bound for eighteen long years, be set free from this bondage on the sabbath day?" 17. When he said this, all his opponents were put to shame; and the entire crowd was rejoicing at all the wonderful things that he was doing.[10]

Later:

> 31. At that very hour some Pharisees came and said to him, "Get away from here, for Herod wants to kill you." 32. He said to them, "Go and tell that fox for me, 'Listen, I am casting out demons and performing cures today and tomorrow, and on the third day I finish my work. 33. Yet today, tomorrow, and the next day I must be on my way, because it is impossible for a prophet to be killed outside of Jerusalem.' "

There is no parallel in the other Gospels to Herod Antipas seeking to kill Jesus.

In an episode recounted only in Luke Jesus confronted the lawyers and the Pharisees (14.1ff.).[11] He was at dinner on the

Sabbath in the house of a prominent Pharisee, and he was being closely watched. A man in front of him suffered from dropsy:

> 14.3. And Jesus asked the lawyers and Pharisees, "Is it lawful to cure people on the sabbath, or not?" 4. But they were silent. So Jesus took him and healed him, and sent him away. 5. Then he said to them, "If one of you has a child or an ox that has fallen into a well, will you not immediately pull it out on a sabbath day?" 6. And they could not reply to this.

On his way to Jerusalem Jesus was acclaimed by the crowd (19.37f.), and the Pharisees asked Jesus to order his disciples to stop (19.39). Jesus replied that if they were quiet the stones would shout out. Again, there is no parallel to the Pharisees' request and Jesus' response. He reached Jerusalem. The cleansing of the Temple is reported without detail (19.45f.). The chief priests, scribes, and leaders of the people looked for a way to kill him, but they could not, for the people were spellbound by him (19.48). When he was teaching in the Temple, the chief priests, scribes, and elders asked by what authority he was doing these things (20.2). His response was as in Mark and Matthew. He told the parable against the scribes and the chief priests: they wanted to seize him then and there, but they feared the people (20.19).

They tried to trap him through spies, and they asked the familiar question about paying taxes to the Romans and got the same response (20.20ff.). The Sadducees posed their question about the woman who successively married seven brothers (20.27ff.). They received the same answer, but, in contrast to Mark and Matthew, it was couched in a gentle and responsive way.

Shortly before the Passover the chief priests and scribes were looking for a way to kill Jesus yet still they were afraid of the people (22.1f.). Judas discussed with the chief priests and officers of the Temple police how to betray Jesus, and they paid him (22.3ff.). After Passover dinner Jesus went with his disciples to the Mount of Olives (22.39). Judas came leading a crowd (22.47). Those around Jesus asked if they should draw their swords, and one cut off the ear of the high priest's slave (22.49ff.). With the crowd were the chief priests, the officers of the Temple police, and the elders of the people who had come for Jesus (22.52).

They seized him and took him to the house of the high priest (22.54). There is no indication in Luke that there was a meeting of the Sanhedrin that night, though Jesus was mocked and beaten (22.63ff.).[12] Then:

> 22.66 When day came, the assembly of the elders of the people, both chief priests and scribes, gathered together, and they brought him to their council. 67. They said, "If you are the Messiah, tell us." He replied, "If I tell you, you will not believe; 68. and if I question you, you will not answer. 69. But from now on the Son of Man will be seated at the right hand of the power of God." 70. All of them asked, "Are you, then, the Son of God?" He said to them, "You say that I am." 71. Then they said, "What further testimony do we need? We have heard it ourselves from his own lips!"

Thus, in the morning there was a trial session before the Sanhedrin. They decided he was guilty, but we are not told that they passed sentence. If they had, that behavior would have been contrary to law, since sentencing had to wait until the following day and there had been no trial during the night.

They took Jesus to Pilate and accused him: he was perverting their nation, forbidding them to pay taxes to the emperor, and claiming that he was the Messiah, a king (23.1f.). Pilate asked Jesus if he were the king of the Jews (23.3). There is, thus, a divergence here from Mark and Matthew, in which Pilate seemed to know beforehand that Jesus was said to be the king of the Jews.

Jesus replied, "You say so," and Pilate found no charge against him.[13] Pilate, as in Mark and Matthew, was reluctant to condemn Jesus, but this time he tried to pass the buck and sent Jesus to Herod Antipas, who was then in Jerusalem (23.6ff.).[14] But Herod sent him back. Pilate still tried to release Jesus, but eventually crucified him. The inscription on the cross read: "This is the king of the Jews" (23.38). So the crime for which he was put to death was maiestas (treason).[15]

5

✠

MARK:
MATTHEW
AND
LUKE

✠ ✠ ✠

IN THE EVENTS LEADING UP TO JESUS' ARREST, THE arrest itself, the trials, and the execution there is a very obvious relationship between Matthew, Mark, and Luke. I accept the standard view that Matthew and Luke used Mark.[1] On that basis, indeed, for those episodes Mark was by far the most important source for Matthew and Luke. They recount the same episodes and in the same order. But there are divergences. Above all, the events in Mark have a dramatic, dynamic tension that is much reduced in Luke and lost in Matthew.

In Mark, Jesus is the charismatic authority who immediately threatens the institutional authority. At the very beginning Jesus is confrontational. He says to the paralytic, "Child, your sins are forgiven you." These are daunting words to the audience, because Jesus has done nothing to justify them. While the scribes are only thinking, but not saying, that the words are blasphemous, Jesus challenges them. Only thereafter does he show his might and cure the paralytic. The Pharisees now follow Jesus about, very understandably, to know what to make of him and even to co-opt him: they watch him eating with sinners in the house of Levi, ask why his disciples do not fast as other religious people do, and ask why his disciples pluck grain on the Sabbath against the law. In none of these episodes are the Pharisees shown as overtly hostile. Nor do they seek to entrap him. Still tracking Jesus, the Pharisees watch to see whether he will cure a withered hand on the Sabbath. Instead of doing so, Jesus puts a direct challenge to the Pharisees; only subsequently does he effect the cure. Jesus' challenge is unfair because, while for the Pharisees it was not lawful to work on the Sabbath, healing need not involve any of the thirty-nine prohibited types of work set out in Mishnah Shabbath 7.2. The Pharisees see that he cannot be co-opted and that he is a threat to them, and they conspire with the Herodians how they might destroy him. They overreact. Still, they continue to track him—scribes come from Jerusalem to see him in Galilee—and Jesus performs more miracles. But it must be remembered that miracle workers were common. The scribes claim that Jesus' power came from Beelzebul: this claim was seen as not implausible, and Jesus' own family thought he had gone mad. He still had not established his authority with the crowd. Jesus preached in his own hometown and offended the congregation. Their lack of belief in him astonished Jesus. Pharisees and scribes who had come from Jerusalem were still trying to understand: they asked why some of his disciples ate without the ritual hand washing. He rounded on them, calling them hypocrites. He mounted an attack on the oral law that the Pharisees observed and told them they abandoned God's commands. Later, the Pharisees, who had not entirely given up on Jesus, asked for a sign from heaven. Jesus refused to oblige.

Considerably later, Jesus enjoyed a triumphant welcome from the crowd as he made his way to Jerusalem. The precise meaning of the acclamation cannot be established, but clearly the crowd accepted that he was a very special person and favored by God. In Jerusalem itself, just before the Passover, in the Temple precincts, Jesus violently obstructed the payment of the Temple tax and the performance of the Passover sacrifices. This was an assault on Pharisees, Sadducees, and all other observing Jews. Unsurprisingly, the chief priests—who for the first time are said to be against Jesus—join the Pharisees in wanting Jesus dead.

But even now, the chief priests, scribes, and elders had not entirely given up on Jesus, and they asked him to tell by what authority he acted as he did. Jesus effectively refused. He then insulted them in a parable. After that they sent Pharisees and Herodians to entrap him, and they asked him the no-win question, whether it was lawful to pay taxes to the Romans. The Sadducees asked a much less dangerous question, really one of little relevance, but Jesus showed he was hostile to them, too. In the Temple Jesus told the people to beware of the scribes. His hostility to them was ever more public. The chief priests and scribes now sought to kill Jesus by stealth, but not during Passover, in case there was an uproar from the people. Judas promised to betray Jesus. Jesus was arrested by a crowd from the chief priests, scribes, and elders and taken to the house of the high priest, where he was tried by the Sanhedrin. The trial was illegal, certainly because it was held at night and probably also because it was held in a private house. Still, despite that illegality, the judges insisted on following the strict rules of evidence, and Jesus could not be convicted. The high priest intervened in an outrageous, bullying way, claiming that they had no need of more witnesses because they had heard Jesus blaspheme; the judges gave way and convicted Jesus. The following morning the Sanhedrin reconvened according to law to confirm the verdict or not and to pass sentence. But the judges had repented of their following the high priest. They did not condemn Jesus but delivered him to the Roman authorities. Pontius Pilate was aware of Jesus and his reputation, and asked if he were the king of the Jews. In the face of Jesus' obduracy, Pilate with regret found him guilty of treason against the emperor and finally executed him by crucifixion.

Matthew follows Mark but fails to realize the dramatic pattern. Thus, when Jesus tells the paralytic that his sins are forgiven, the scribes say among themselves that Jesus blasphemes. Jesus is no longer confrontational: the scribes initiate the dispute. Then the Pharisees are not shown as so eager in tracking Jesus as they are in the remainder of Mark 2. The three episodes are recounted, but it is the disciples of John the Baptist, not the Pharisees, who ask why Jesus' disciples do not fast. The significance of the Pharisees' interest in Jesus is diminished. And the third episode, when Jesus is asked why his disciples pluck grain on the Sabbath, is recounted in Matthew in a context remote from the others. Again, when Jesus cures the withered hand in Matthew, it is no longer he but the Pharisees who start the argument. In further episodes there is no subtext that people were so doubtful of Jesus that even his relatives thought he had gone mad. People were more accepting of Jesus, and at an earlier point, than they were in Mark. Jesus was tried illegally at night and in a private house by the Sanhedrin and condemned. But at the morning session the conviction does not seem to have been withdrawn.

Luke also follows Mark but with variations. These variations are not always those found in Matthew. Again, when Jesus tells the paralytic that his sins are forgiven, the Pharisees say that he blasphemes. It is the Pharisees, more clearly than in Mark, who ask why his disciples do not fast. The confrontation over the withered hand proceeds from Jesus as in Mark. Only in Luke do the Pharisees warn Jesus that Herod Antipas wants to kill him. In Luke there was no illegal trial of Jesus by the Sanhedrin at night, but there was the first stage of a trial the following morning. In all three Synoptic Gospels Pilate is shown as extremely reluctant to condemn Jesus. But only in Matthew does his wife appeal to him to have nothing to do with this innocent man.[2] And only in Luke does Pilate pass the buck and send Jesus to Herod Antipas.[3]

The differences between Matthew and Luke here are particularly important for the history of early Christianity. Matthew and Luke both take Mark as their main source for these events, but when they diverge from him, they sometimes differ between themselves. How can that be? The explanation is obviously not that they had another common source for these matters. That would account for their divergences from Mark, but not for the differences between themselves. Nor can it be that in this regard they each had another source that was not available to the other. That would not explain why in large measure they differ from Mark at the same points. The only explanation is that in the community or communities in which Matthew and Luke were written, Mark was the main narrative source for the events leading up to Jesus' arrest, the arrest, trials, and execution, but aspects of Mark's account were the subject of considerable controversy, and various solutions were proffered.

The outlines of the controversy can be traced. One opinion was that Jesus was less confrontational and belligerent toward the Pharisees than he appears in Mark. The Pharisees were thought to be less interested in tracking Jesus before the cleansing of the Temple, to see whether he could be co-opted or was a fraud. The ordinary people were believed to be more accepting of Jesus than they are represented in Mark. Again, there was a difference of opinion over Jesus appearing before the chief priests and the Pharisees. Some held, as we find in Luke, that there was no illegal meeting of the Sanhedrin at night. Others went even farther than Mark: not only, as we see in Matthew, did the Sanhedrin meet at night but it deliberately sought false evidence and renewed the conviction the following morning. Again, there were those who held that Pilate was even more reluctant to execute Jesus than appears in Mark. This resulted in Pilate's wife intervening for Jesus in Matthew. In Luke Pilate even tried to pass the buck by sending Jesus, for unnecessary jurisdictional reasons, to Herod Antipas. (The difference of opinion in Matthew and Luke as to who asked Jesus why his disciples did not fast I would attribute simply to Mark's latent ambiguity.)

Thus, though Matthew and Luke differ, they have a common trend away from Mark, though this is perhaps less apparent in Luke. They show Jesus as less belligerent toward the Pharisees, the Pharisees as less interested in co-opting Jesus, the ordinary people as more sympathetic to Jesus, and Pilate as even less willing to execute Jesus. Matthew shows the Sanhedrin in a rather worse light.

One reason for the writing of Matthew and Luke was to react against the narrative tradition in Mark. Can we, accordingly, decide in favor of the accuracy of one version rather than another? One argument that we cannot use is that there are illogicalities in Matthew and Luke that do not appear in Mark. The illogicalities are the result of the other two Synoptic Gospels following, but changing, Mark and failing to make enough changes. This is no evidence that the changes that were made were not closer to the truth and were made for that reason. Nor is it necessarily an argument in favor of Mark that there the drama of the unfolding events is more dynamic. To heighten the drama, Mark might consciously or unconsciously have imposed artificialities which Matthew and Luke later corrected.

Despite the last two sentences I do, in fact, tend to believe that the drama in Mark is closer to the original. The events were dramatic. Moreover, in other regards Mark shows a greater understanding, perhaps because he was closer to them. One example of Mark's better understanding is Peter's denial of Jesus (Mark 14.66ff.). David Daube points out that a Jew must not deny his Jewishness when questioned by a Gentile, even at the risk of his life. The rabbis, Daube observed, make two basic distinctions: first between evasion and a straight no; second between a private and a public action.[4] Exactly this pattern is found in Peter's three denials of Jesus in Mark 14.66ff. Peter first says to the maidservant, "I neither know nor understand what you say." This is an evasion in private. She follows him and says to others, "This is one of them." Peter evades again, but this time in public. Bystanders ask him if he is not one with Jesus, and Peter says, "I do not know the man of whom you speak." This is an outright public denial. Daube points out that Matthew's version (26.69ff.) is further from the rabbinic categories—all three denials are public; the first evasive, the second and third direct. Luke (22.54ff.) does not appreciate the rabbinic categories at all: all three denials are public, the first two are direct, the third an evasion. In John 18.25ff., all three denials are direct and in public. Daube is reluctant to claim that Mark is historically accurate.[5]

The central issue for us is the nature of the trial proceedings, if any, before the Sanhedrin, and here in the three Synoptics we have three very different versions, all of which show the Sanhedrin acting in an illegal way. The one indisputable fact about Jesus' life is that he was executed by the Romans in a Roman manner, crucifixion, for a secular Roman crime, sedition or treason. If the Sanhedrin had condemned Jesus to death for a religious crime, it would be for Jews to carry out the sentence. Yet in Matthew the Sanhedrin condemns Jesus, so the Romans should not carry out the execution in a non-Jewish way. There is no reason for the Sanhedrin not to carry out the sentence. As we shall see in chapter 8, they had the power to do so. And Pilate, it must be stressed, is most reluctant to be involved. In Luke, the Sanhedrin finds Jesus guilty of blasphemy on the morning after his arrest. But having gone to that trouble, it does not wait to reconvene the following day to confirm the verdict and to pass sentence. Instead, they hand him over to Pilate with accusations that he was perverting their nation, forbidding them to pay taxes, and claiming to be a king. Again it must be stressed that Pilate was most reluctant to get involved. The scenario in Luke is possible, but very implausible. In Mark, the Sanhedrin convicts Jesus in the illegal trial at night but reverses itself in the morning. So it could not execute Jesus. It hands Jesus over to Pilate with accusations, and Pilate tries him and, still with much hesitation, executes him for a secular crime. Only the version in Mark can both account for the course of events and be plausible. I conclude that it is more likely to be close to the truth than the versions in Matthew and Luke. I therefore discount Matthew and Luke as evidence of the main course of events leading up to the execution of Jesus. Still, that does not mean that, in points of detail, one or the other may not be more accurate than Mark. Nor am I suggesting that the tradition that did not fully accept Mark's version was in any way being deliberately misleading.

What I should like to suggest is that though we cannot establish with any degree of precision the cities where Matthew, Mark, and Luke were compiled, and though likewise it is hard to be precise about the nature of the community for which each was written, nonetheless Mark is closer to an understanding of proceedings before the Sanhedrin, possibly because it is earlier in date before a sharp separation had occurred between Jews and Christians.[6]

It should be noted in passing, and will be discussed later in chapter 9, that nothing in any of the four Gospels suggests that Pilate's reluctance to execute Jesus had anything to do with sympathy.

I wish to point out the contrast among the three Synoptics over Jesus' trials. In Mark the Sanhedrin tried Jesus for blasphemy (Mark 14.53ff.), the witnesses were insufficient in their testimony (Mark 14.56ff.), the high priest intervened saying they had heard blasphemy (Mark 14.63), and the judges found him guilty (Mark 14.64). At the necessary meeting the following morning they did not confirm their sentence, but they took Jesus to Pilate, who asked him if he were the king of the Jews (Mark 15.1ff.). So Pilate was investigating a secular crime against the Romans. In Matthew, in contrast, the witnesses were sufficient (Matthew 26.60f.), though the high priest also intervened violently (Matthew 26.63ff.). From the episode with Judas (Matthew 27.3ff.) we know that at the morning session (Matthew 27.1), Matthew accepted that the judges had condemned Jesus. The evidence, though, is so indirect that we may suspect that it was the evangelist's opinion that the Sanhedrin had convicted but that this was not clear in his sources. The judges delivered him to Pilate, who questioned Jesus on the same secular issue as in Mark. In Luke there was only a morning session (Luke 22.66ff.). There is no emphasis on lack of witnesses: the stress is all on whether Jesus claimed to be the Messiah. The Sanhedrin took Jesus before Pilate and accused him: "We found this man perverting our nation, forbidding us to pay taxes to the emperor, and saying that he himself is the Messiah, a king" (Luke 23.3). Of these three accusations before the Roman procurator, the first is of the religious offense of leading a town astray and this, according to Mishnah Sanhedrin 7.4, is punishable by death by stoning. Perverting the Jewish nation is no crime against Roman law.[7] The third accusation as it is recorded is also primarily of a religious offense. But Pilate's interest is in the Roman crime of sedition, and he asks Jesus if he is the king of the Jews (Luke 23.2).

In this contrast, only Mark tells the story plausibly. Thus, in Matthew, there was no need (as there was in Mark) for the high priest to rend his garment inappropriately and illegally: he already had the necessary witnesses. In Luke it was pointless to have the Sanhedrin accuse Jesus of a purely religious offense in front of Pilate. In so far as Matthew and Luke here depend on Mark, they have again weakened the dynamics of the course of events, due to a lack of understanding. We can be confident that we do not this time have an instance where Mark has deliberately heightened the drama, whereas Matthew or Luke is closer to the original tradition. It is in Matthew that the high priest's tearing of his clothes is quite pointless though dramatic; in Mark it has a fundamental role. It is Luke that shows the Sanhedrin irrelevantly and uselessly charging Jesus with religious crimes before Pilate.

Though this book is not a commentary on the structure of Mark, the tightness of its construction, compared to that of Matthew and Luke, will surface again in various important ways. At the end of this chapter, therefore, I wish to draw attention to one further illustration, the episode in Galilee when his mother and brothers came to find Jesus. In Mark, this is linked with the opinion that he had gone mad: close relatives were to be the guardians of the insane. Some said, "He has an unclean spirit" (Mark 3.30). Then Jesus' relatives appear, and the people tell him so (Mark 3.31ff.). Jesus responds, "Whoever does the will of God is my brother and sister and mother" (Mark 3.35). Jesus is skillfully dismissing the idea of guardianship by his natural relatives. The same episode appears in Luke 8.19ff., but there is no claim in the context that anyone believes that Jesus is insane: the episode loses most of its point.

6

✝

MARK
AND
JOHN

✝ ✝ ✝

WE CAN NOW FOCUS ATTENTION PRIMARILY ON MARK
and John, and the issue is still plausibility of the traditions.[1] The
two Gospels are each internally consistent but they are irreconcilable.

Still, they do have features in common. In both, Jesus is
more confrontational than in the other two Synoptic Gospels.
In Mark, at the beginning of his ministry, Jesus is aggressive
toward the scribes/Pharisees. In John, at the beginning, Jesus'
behavior toward Pharisees, Sadducees, and other observing Jews
is hostile in the extreme, but thereafter his main opponents are
the Pharisees. In both Gospels, the Pharisees at first act with
very considerable restraint. In both, the Sanhedrin does not
convict Jesus.

Apart from the issue of a trial before the Sanhedrin there are
several major differences in the narratives in Mark and John.
For all of these Mark is plausible, John is implausible.

In Mark the so-called cleansing of the Temple was at the end of Jesus' ministry, in John at the outset. By any standard Jesus' behavior was outrageous and deeply offensive to Sadducees, who were the main guardians of the Temple, to Pharisees, who were more interested in law and ritual, and to other observing Jews. It is to me inconceivable that anyone who had not previously publicly shown supernatural powers could act in such a way without dire consequences.[2] He would have been attacked or stopped on the spot. But in John nothing happens to Jesus as a result. We are not even told of the reaction to his behavior. Yet John makes Jesus behave more violently than does Mark. The cleansing of the Temple fits much better late in Jesus' ministry when people knew of his achievements. Yet even so, in Mark, it leads on to Jesus' arrest.

The Last Supper in Mark is a Passover dinner (Mark 14.12–26), but in John Jesus is crucified before Passover, hence the Last Supper could not be a celebration of Passover. Again, Mark's account is plausible, John's is not. The Last Supper, as we shall see, was a Passover feast.

The Last Supper is also portrayed in Matthew 26 as a Passover meal. The disciples ask him where he would like them to prepare his Passover dinner, he gives instructions, and they prepare for Passover (Matthew 26.17–19). After dinner they sing the Passover Hymn and go to the Mount of Olives (Matthew 26.30). A very similar account is in Luke (22.1–39), which even has Jesus saying, "How I have longed to eat this Passover with you before my death!" (Luke 22.15).

In contrast, there is none of this in John. We are told, "Now before the Passover feast Jesus knew that his hour had come that he must leave this world and go to the Father" (13.1).[3] Then comes the Last Supper (13.2ff.). Jesus is crucified, and we are told, "Because it was the eve of Passover, the Jews were anxious that the bodies should not remain on the cross" (19.31). In no way could the Last Supper be a Passover meal in John.

But that the meal was Passover dinner is fundamental for Jesus as Messiah, whose ministry is above all to the Jews. Once more there is a basic problem in timing. Raymond Brown is forced to conclude that "for unknown reasons, on Thursday evening, the 14th of Nisan by the official calendar, the day before Passover, Jesus ate with his disciples a meal that had Passover characteristics."[4] This is most unconvincing. The one Gospel, John, that puts the Last Supper before the Passover has a dinner that has no specifically Passover characteristics. Brown's view would force us to hold that a source of John cut out from the tradition the Passover characteristics of the Last Supper, that a source of the Synoptics altered the time of the Last Supper to make it a Passover feast, and that Jesus and his disciples ate a last meal that had Passover characteristics but was not Passover "for unknown reasons." It is much simpler to hold with Joachim Jeremias that the Last Supper was a Passover dinner.[5] Again, the timing in John has been altered. Why? If one accepts the existence of S, the Pharisaic narrative source that I suggest was used in John, there is no problem. A prime purpose of the S tradition is to separate Jesus, miracle worker though he is, from the Jews and their religious rituals. For S, and hence for John, Jesus should not be represented as celebrating the Passover.[6]

Some scholars do believe that they see in John 13.21–30 traces of the Last Supper as a Passover meal.[7] This would suit my case that the Last Supper was accurately portrayed in the Synoptics as a Passover meal and that the timing in John 19.31 has been altered because of the use of S, which portrayed the Last Supper otherwise. But the evidence seems to be inconclusive and unpersuasive. The main argument must be that in all four Gospels (Matthew 26.20; Mark 14.18; Luke 22.14; John 13.12, 23, 25) the participants are represented as reclining ($\alpha\nu\alpha\kappa\epsilon\iota\mu\alpha\iota$ is the verb used), not as sitting. Yet sitting was usual at meals. For Jeremias: "It is *absolutely impossible* that Jesus and his disciples should have *reclined* at table for their ordinary meals. How is it then that they recline at table in the case of the Last Supper? There can be only one answer: at the passover meal it was a *ritual duty* to recline at table as a symbol of freedom, also, as it is expressly stated, for 'the poorest man in Israel.' "[8] This goes too far. Reclining was obligatory at a Passover meal,[9] but it was also usual at a party or a feast.[10] Thus, when the woman poured ointment on Jesus' head he was "reclining" at table in the house of Simon the leper (Mark 14.3). Likewise at the house of Levi, Jesus and many tax collectors and sinners reclined at dinner. And the Last Supper was certainly a more important occasion for Jesus than these. No more conclusive is Jeremias's correct observation that in John the Last Supper was eaten in a state of levitical purity (13.10).[11] That was no doubt usual for eating the Passover lamb, but was also usual on other special occasions. More to the point, the rabbinic sources do not support the notion that it was necessary to eat the Passover lamb in a state of levitical purity.[12]

A second detail from the Last Supper important for us is the Eucharist itself. At the end of the meal Jesus took bread, broke it, gave it to the disciples, and said, "Take, eat: this is my body" (Matthew 26.26; Mark 14.22; Luke 22.19). As David Daube insists, if there had been no precedent for this, "his disciples—to put it mildly—would have been perplexed."[13] And he convincingly shows that the precedent was in the Passover liturgy.[14] In the liturgy, prior to the meal a portion of unleavened bread is broken off, taken from the table, and brought back at the end of the meal and distributed to the company as the last bit of food that night. Traditionally, this piece of bread is called Aphiqoman. The word is not Semitic but the Greek ἀφικόμενος or ἐφικόμενος, and means "the coming one," or "he that cometh," and represents the Messiah. When Jesus at the finale of the meal breaks bread and says, "Take, eat: this is my body," he is saying to the disciples, "I am the Messiah." The Eucharist appears in Matthew, Mark, and Luke, and it is in the highest degree significant that it is entirely absent from John. For S, the Last Supper must in no way appear as a Passover meal: Jesus' participation in Jewish ritual is suppressed. The detail was not in S, and the redactor has not inserted it. The Eucharist element in the Synoptic Gospels but not in John and its connection with the Aphiqoman is for me the final proof that the Synoptics correctly show the Last Supper as a Passover meal.[15]

We can go further. Eucharistic details do appear in John at 6.50–58, as we have seen, in a context which is not Passover or the Last Supper, but in the synagogue at Capernaum (6.59), and in which they do cause confusion and horror or anger. Jesus declared he was the living bread come down from heaven and that the bread he would give for the life of the world was his flesh. "The Jews then disputed among themselves, saying, 'How can this man give us his flesh to eat?'" (6.52). Jesus responded, saying inter alia that those who ate his flesh and drank his blood might have everlasting life, but otherwise they would have no life in them (6.53ff.). Many of his disciples found this teaching offensive: "Because of this many of his disciples turned back and no longer went about with him" (6.66). Thus, Eucharistic details outside of Passover in John are both mystifying and horrifying; in the Synoptics in the Last Supper they cause no surprise. The contrast shows that there can be no doubt that at the Last Supper as Passover in the Synoptics Jesus was revealing himself as the Aphiqoman, the Messiah. Thus, the timing of the Last Supper in John is inaccurate.

The one episode in the Gospels that we can be sure did not occur is the raising of Lazarus from the dead. It is by far the most important, detailed miracle. If it had occurred it would have been deeply embedded in the tradition from the start and, of necessity, would have appeared in all four Gospels. But it is encountered only in John. Raymond Brown has a rather different perspective:

> From the contents of the Johannine account, then, there is no conclusive reason for assuming that the skeleton of the story does not stem from early tradition about Jesus. What causes doubt is the importance that John gives to the raising of Lazarus as the cause for Jesus' death. We suggest that here we have another instance of the pedagogical genius of the Fourth Gospel.[16]

For me, it is not the contents of the Johannine account that proves that it was not part of the early tradition but its absence from the other Gospels, coupled with its overreaching significance. This absence from the Synoptics has, of course, long been noticed by scholars. One common suggestion, rebutted by Brown, is that the story of the raising of Lazarus is a fictional composition based on Synoptic material: it is inspired, it is said, by the story of the raising of the widow's son at Nain (Luke 7.11–16), the characters taken from Luke 10.38–42, and the parable of Lazarus (Luke 16.19–31). But Brown correctly emphasizes that this opinion is based on an approach that has not been successful elsewhere in understanding John, namely, that John is dependent on the Synoptics and does not contain material from a different historical tradition.

It is precisely the importance of the raising of Lazarus for the death of Jesus that persuades me that one can uncover something about this different historical tradition for John. Martha met Jesus, then returned home to fetch Mary. There were Jews in the house comforting her (11.31), and they followed Mary because they thought she was going to the tomb to weep (11.31). They witnessed the resurrection of Lazarus, and many of them came to believe in Jesus (11.45).[17] But some did not, and they told the Pharisees what Jesus had done (11.46). The chief priests and the Pharisees, we are told, called a special meeting of the Sanhedrin (11.47). There is something significantly inaccurate in this because the Pharisees as such had no power to summon the council, though most of the scribes—professional lawyers and one of the three orders of the Sanhedrin—were Pharisees.[18] The elite priests, though, were Sadducees. Brown plausibly suggests that the Sanhedrin would not have moved against Jesus if the Pharisees had not been against him.[19] At the Sanhedrin it was argued, "If we leave him thus alone, all men will believe in him, and the Romans will come and take away both our place ($\tau o\pi o\varsigma$) and the nation ($\breve{\epsilon}\theta\nu o\varsigma$)" (11.48). Caiaphas declared: "You know nothing. Nor do you take into account that it is expedient that one man should die for the people and that the whole nation should not perish" (11.50). This John declares to be a prophesy that Jesus should die for the nation, and not for the nation alone, but also that Jesus will gather together the children of God who had been scattered abroad (11.51f.). From that day the Sanhedrin took counsel together to put Jesus to death (11.53).

If some people at the time believed that Jesus had raised Lazarus from the dead, then the Sanhedrin was perfectly justified in its view. The Romans would have, indeed, come and taken away the place—whether $\tau o\pi o\varsigma$ designates Jerusalem or the Temple—and the nation.[20] This as often was a time of trouble with the Jews for the Romans. Bar Abbas who is described as a "notorious prisoner" (Matthew 27.16) was apparently a terrorist (Mark 15.7; Luke 23.19), and so probably were the two brigands or plunderers—not simply "thieves"[21]—crucified with Jesus.[22] If Jesus raised one man from the dead, he could raise an army. This miracle was a supreme challenge to the Romans. If Jesus were widely thought to be the Messiah, there would be a full-scale insurrection of the Jews, one that the Romans could not allow the Jews to win. If Jesus were thought to be the Messiah but was not, the result of the insurrection would indeed be to the Jews the loss of the τοπος, the Temple or Jerusalem or both, and the nation. It is entirely in keeping with this that the raising of Lazarus was the last miracle in John before Jesus was greeted by a large crowd shouting, "Blessed is the one who comes in the name of the Lord—the King of Israel" (12.13).

John 11.48 is, I believe, a clear reminiscence of the fact that in A.D. 70 the Romans did take away the place and the nation from the Jews as a consequence of another religious uprising. It is written with hindsight.

That there could be a genuine fear of an uprising if Jesus was the Messiah must be stressed. Josephus relates that Herod became alarmed that the eloquence of John the Baptist would lead to some form of sedition, so he struck first before the Baptist's preaching could lead to an uprising.[23] John the Baptist stressed that he himself was not the Messiah,[24] so how much greater would the danger be if Jesus were so regarded?

If we now consider the purpose of the source for John's account of the raising of Lazarus and the reaction of the Sanhedrin up to verse 48, we see that it is to justify fully the role of the Pharisees and the Sanhedrin in bringing about the execution of Jesus. Jesus is for them a very great and pressing danger. In so far as this source justifies the Sanhedrin and the Pharisees it is unsympathetic to Christianity.

It is important to me that I have shown, I believe, John's implausibility and Mark's corresponding plausibility for these episodes without stressing any tendency in John or Mark or any purpose for which the narrative parts of these Gospels may have been written. I have two reasons. First, on the central issue, the role of the Sanhedrin and the involvement of the Romans, neither the account in Mark nor that in John can be shown to be more plausible on its face. Second, to have argued the implausibility of John for these episodes on the basis of any tendency, and then to have used that conclusion to come to a further conclusion on the central issue, would have been to weight the evidence.

IT MAY BE CLAIMED, PERHAPS WITH REASON, THAT to assess the plausibility of Mark, it was inappropriate for me to restrict my gaze to the events leading up to and including the arrest, the trials, and the execution of Jesus. All the narrative events, it may be suggested, should be tested for plausibility before one can estimate what happened at Jesus' trial. This argument may seem all the stronger when we take into account the standard view that Matthew and Luke are much better constructed than Mark whereas, in the events that I have so far described, Mark displays a dramatic, dynamic power that is quite lost in Matthew and weakened in Luke. And Mark devotes a disproportionately large amount of space to the Passion.

In this chapter two other characteristics of Mark will be considered: the emphasis on the fact of Jesus' teaching, coupled with the lack of stress on what actually was publicly taught;

and the emphasis on miracles that Jesus then seems to down-play. Though they do not go directly to the issue of plausibility, they cast much light on Mark's reasons for writing and hence indirectly provide a test for plausibility.

Jesus recruited disciples (1.16ff.).

> 1.21. They went to Capernaum; and when the sabbath came, he entered the synagogue and taught. 22. They were astounded at his teaching, for he taught them as one having authority, and not as the scribes. 23. Just then there was in their synagogue a man with an unclean spirit, 24. and he cried out, "What have you to do with us, Jesus of Naza-reth? Have you come to destroy us? I know who you are, the Holy One of God." 25. But Jesus rebuked him, say-ing, "Be silent, and come out of him!" 26. And the unclean spirit, convulsing him and crying with a loud voice, came out of him. 27. They were all amazed, and they kept on asking one another, "What is this? A new teaching—with authority! He commands even the unclean spirits, and they obey him." 28. At once his fame began to spread through-out the surrounding region of Galilee.

Jesus taught in the synagogue as one having authority and not as the scribes. What the teaching was is not stated. We can re-construct the scribes' style of teaching from the later Mishnah: disputes with one another over details, reliance on past scribes in order to proceed one step forward, refined exegesis and develop-ment from the actual wording of Scripture. The implication here in Mark is that Jesus was his own authority. He did not discuss minute details, did not rely on past scribes, did not always argue from the actual words of Scripture but from a higher meaning. An illustration may be drawn from his response to the question why his disciples plucked grain on the Sabbath (2.23ff.). His first response was to use haggadah, which would in no way carry weight with the Pharisees. But then comes a break with tradition: "The Sabbath was made on account of man, and not man on account of the Sabbath" (2.27). He thus was simply sweeping away centuries of reasoning on the precise nature of prohibited work on the Sabbath. There is no denial of the Sabbath but a rejection of the reasoning used by the Pharisees to establish what amounted to work. But then he produces the real argument from his own authority: "So the Son of man is lord also of the Sabbath" (2.28). Returning to the scene at 1.23ff. we find that Jesus casts out a devil as the result of a few words, and the crowd is amazed and exclaims, "What is this? A new teaching—with authority! He commands even the unclean spirits, and they obey him." The teaching with authority involved the miracle itself, or the miracle confirmed the authority of the teaching. In either event, the miracle was part of the teaching with authority.

In the next few verses he cures a woman with fever (1.30f.), heals many who suffered from various diseases, and casts out demons (1.32ff.). In the morning he goes out by himself to pray, and his disciples tell him that everyone is looking for him (1.35ff.). He replies, "Let us go elsewhere into the neighboring towns, that I may proclaim my message there also. For this purpose I came forth" (1.38). Then he proclaims this message in the synagogues throughout Galilee, and he casts out devils (1.39). Again we are told nothing of the nature of Jesus' message. But in the narrative the teaching is interwoven with casting out devils.

A leper asks if Jesus will heal him (1.40). In anger Jesus touches him and says, "I am willing. Be cleansed" (1.41). The leper is cured, and Jesus orders him to tell no one, but in accordance with the law of Moses he should show himself to the priest and make the appropriate offerings (1.43f.).[1] "In anger": I accept the manuscript ὀργισθείς, not that of other manuscripts σπλαγχισθείς "in pity," on the principle of *difficilior lectio*. It is understandable that an original "in anger" would be changed to "in pity," but not vice versa. Moreover, if "in pity" had been the original reading, it would be surprising that no trace of it survives in Matthew 8.2–4 or in Luke 5.12–14.[2] But then it has to be admitted that no explanation for Jesus' anger is satisfactory especially because his act was full of pity. It cannot be because the leper had broken God's command not to approach others,[3] because Jesus was about to make himself unclean according to the same law by touching the leper.[4] Nor can it be that the leper lacked respect, because he begged Jesus and knelt before him (1.40).[5] Nor was the leper's greeting so brusque as to justify anger. In any event, Mark usually gives only what is needed for the narrative, and words of greeting that were spoken may have been omitted. Indeed, nothing indicates Jesus' anger was with the leper. Perhaps Jesus was angered at being asked to perform a miracle. More importantly, Jesus' fidelity to the law of Moses was strong enough that he ordered the leper to show himself to the priest, as was commanded, and to make the appropriate offerings. But, in contrast to what had gone before, Jesus told the former leper in strong terms not to say anything about the cure to anyone (1.44). Such secrecy is common in Mark. The man disobeyed, and Jesus could no longer go about in a town openly but stayed out in the country (1.45). Jesus' desire for secrecy is again expressed, but it is not explained. Still, many did come to see him.

At the beginning of Mark 2 we have the episode, seen more than once before in this book, of the curing of the paralytic who was let down through the roof. This time our interest is that Jesus' message is embedded in the miracle. He says, "But so that you [plural] may know that the Son of man has authority on earth to forgive sins [he addresses the paralytic] I say to you [singular], stand up, take your mat and go home" (2.10f.). It is worthy of note that before the cure Jesus "was speaking the word to them" (2.2). But what that word was we are not told.

After this, he goes out beside the sea and teaches a great crowd (2.13). But what he tells them we do not know. When Jesus eats in the house of Levi, his disciples are asked why he dines with publicans and sinners (2.15ff.). His reply is: "Those who are well have no need of a physician, but those who are sick: I have come to call not the righteous, but sinners" (2.17). The answer is puzzling. The first part is a commonplace and is banal. It is the linking of the two parts that is puzzling. If, as seems in general, part of Jesus' message is that righteousness in the traditional Jewish sense was not enough but that belief in him was required, then his call should not be restricted to sinners.[6] And that he has "come to call" implies that he has a very special role. The nature of that call is not stated: nothing expressed in the text justifies the assumption in the King James Version that it is a call to repentance. When Jesus is asked why his disciples do not fast (2.18ff.), his reply is only to the effect that he is like a bridegroom to the disciples. As for their plucking grain on the Sabbath, his response is twofold: first that the Pharisaic interpretation of the prohibition of work on the Sabbath is misguided, second that the Son of man is lord even of the Sabbath.

For our present purposes, what these three episodes have in common is only that Jesus is claiming to be a very special person in a religious sense (unless Son of man can be given a technical meaning). What is religiously special about him is not made clear. None of these episodes involves a miracle: Jesus is insisting that he is special, without invoking miracles. When he cures the withered hand in the synagogue on the Sabbath (3.1ff.), he makes the same claim about the nature of the Sabbath prohibition, but he does not add that he is lord over the Sabbath.

Jesus cured many (3.7ff.), and he was followed by such a crowd who wanted to be healed that he had a boat made ready to escape the crush. Though this is not stated quite explicitly, he cast out devils. This appears from the fact that those with unclean spirits fell down before him exclaiming, "You are the Son of God" (3.11). But he warned them not to make him known (3.12). Though he did cure those who asked him, he seemed not to want to be pursued as a miracle worker. Yet he then appointed twelve disciples to proclaim the message and gave them authority to cast out demons (3.14). But again, what the message was is not stated.

The scribes who had come from Jerusalem said he had Beelzebul and could cast out evil spirits by the power of the devil (3.22). He responded:

3.28. "Truly, I tell you that all sins and blasphemies will be forgiven to the sons of men, whatever they may blaspheme. 29. But whoever blasphemes against the Holy Spirit has never forgiveness, but is liable of an eternal sin." 30. Because they said, "He has an unclean spirit."

Thus, no forgiveness was possible for blasphemy against the Holy Spirit, and Jesus equated himself with the Holy Spirit.

Jesus taught a large crowd beside the sea (4.1ff.), but only in incomprehensible parables. Not even the disciples understood, but they asked him about the parables when he was alone (4.10). His reply was truly astonishing. Jesus told them they had been given the mystery of the kingdom of God. But to those outside, all things were to be told in parables so they would see but not perceive, and hear but not understand, in order that they would not turn and be forgiven (4.11f.). Jesus was saying that he was deliberately couching his message so that it would not be understood. Then he explained to the disciples, but only to the disciples, what he meant by the parable of the seed falling on different kinds of ground (4.13ff.). Again, it is emphasized that he spoke to the crowd only in parables, but explained everything in private to his disciples (4.33). Then he showed the disciples that even the storm and the wind obeyed him.

(Jesus' insistence that he speaks incomprehensibly quite deliberately so that his hearers will not understand, will not turn, and so will not be forgiven, presents serious theologians with serious theological problems. The explanations are various, but most have standard prime features. Thus, it is insisted that Jesus' words must not be taken at face value; and it is precisely this insistence in the Gospel that concerns me. The theologians' argument is that those who do not accept Jesus' message are not just resisting, but in a profound sense they lack understanding; to explain this, the incomprehension is claimed to be built into the divine message. But there are difficulties with this approach. On a theological level, a prime difficulty is that no one, not even the disciples, understand. Even when Jesus explains a parable privately, they continue to misunderstand his next words. Moreover, I fail to see why his words should not be taken at face value, at least on one level. After all, at this point Jesus is no longer talking in parables but explaining why he talks in parables. And a theological explanation should not stress the crowd's resisting Jesus' message—resistance is not indicated in the texts—but account for his strong desire not to be understood. That desire, after all, is precisely what is expressed).

He removed a legion of unclean spirits from a man and sent them into a herd of pigs (5.1ff.). He told the man to tell his friends what things he had done for him. Everyone marveled (5.20). He cured a woman who had been hemorrhaging for twelve years (5.25ff.). He raised Jairus's daughter from the dead

(5.22–24; 5.35–43). But he ordered that no one should know about it.

He went about the villages teaching, but we are told nothing of the nature of the teaching. He gave instructions to his disciples, and they cast out demons (6.7ff.).

Jesus performed the miracle of feeding the multitude with five loaves and two fish (6.30ff.). After that, he walked on water (6.47ff.). At Genneraset where they landed, many followed him: the sick who touched the fringe of his cloak were healed (6.53ff.).

Pharisees and scribes had come from Jerusalem and they asked Jesus why his disciples ate with unwashed hands (7.1ff.). Jesus upbraided them, teaching that they abandoned God's law to follow human precepts. He condemned the oral law followed by the Pharisees. Then he told the crowd that nothing outside a person defiles by going in, but that what comes out defiles (7.14f.). Again, this teaching is incomprehensible on its face. But Jesus explained privately to the disciples who had asked the meaning (7.17ff.). It is not the food that one eats that defiles. Thus, there would be no food taboos, a complete contradiction of express Mosaic law. Instead, what defiles are evil thoughts: fornication, theft, murder, and so on.

Jesus went to Tyre, where a Gentile woman of Syrophoenician origin asked him to cure her daughter (7.24ff.). Jesus refused in very rough language, saying in effect that his mission was to the Jews. She turned aside his refusal, and Jesus relented. In the Decapolis, Jesus cured one who was deaf and dumb (7.31ff.), but ordered those around to tell no one.

Jesus again fed a crowd with seven loaves and a few fish (8.1ff.). He told his disciples to beware of the yeast of the Pharisees and of Herod (8.14ff.). They thought he was talking about their not having bread. Jesus said to them, "Do you still not understand?" (8.21).

Jesus cured a blind man and sent him home, but told him not even to go into the village (8.22ff.). Thus, again, Jesus wanted a miracle kept secret.

Some time later occurred the Transfiguration (9.2ff.). He ordered the disciples to tell no one until the Son of man had risen from the dead (9.9).

Jesus cast out an unclean spirit that the disciples could not cast out, and attributed it to the power of prayer (9.14ff.).

Jesus taught that Moses allowed men to divorce their wives as a concession to the hardness of their hearts and that there should be no divorce (10.2ff.). Subsequently, he explained his reason privately to his disciples (10.10ff.). He further taught that whoever has not received the kingdom of God as a little child would not enter it (10.15). He also taught how hard it was for the wealthy to enter heaven (10.17ff.).

Jesus cured blind Bartimaeus (10.46). He cursed and withered a fig tree (11.20ff.). After he cleansed the Temple he taught a parable against the chief priests, scribes, and elders (12.1ff.), and this they did understand. He taught the Sadducees that those who rise from the dead do not marry (12.18ff.). And he taught a scribe that the greatest commandment is to love God with all one's might and to love one's neighbor as oneself (12.28ff.).

Thus, Mark stresses Jesus' enormous talents as a teacher—a teacher with authority—and as a miracle worker. Miracles are, indeed, often intertwined with Jesus' message, even an integral part of it. But Mark's account has two rather unexpected characteristics which demand explanation. First, Jesus often insists that no one be told of a miracle that he has just performed.[7] Second, he teaches with authority but, for the most part, we are not told what his message is. Even when we are told what he taught, the teaching is usually in the form of parables, the understanding of which is difficult.

A standard explanation of Jesus wanting to hide some of his miracles is that miracle workers were common and Jesus did not want to be regarded as merely or even as primarily a miracle worker. That the danger was real is shown at 9.38ff.:

> John said to him, "Teacher, we saw someone casting out demons in your name, and we tried to stop him, because he was not following us." 39. But Jesus said, "Do not stop him; for no one who does a deed of power in my name will be able soon afterward to speak evil of me. 40. Whoever is not against us is for us. 41. For truly I tell you, whoever gives you a cup of water to drink because you bear the name of Christ will by no means lose the reward.

Thus, not only was Jesus' work in driving out demons imitated, but the imitator acted in the name of Jesus. For Jesus this was permissible, not because the other miracle worker was a believer but because to use Jesus' name when performing his cures would obstruct that man from speaking out against Jesus.[8] The practice of working miracles in his name continued even after Jesus' death:

> Acts 19.13. Then some itinerant Jewish exorcists tried to use the name of the Lord Jesus over those who had evil spirits, saying, "I abjure you by the Jesus whom Paul proclaims." 14. Seven sons of a Jewish high priest named Sceva were doing this. 15. But the evil spirit said to them in reply, "Jesus I know, and Paul I know, but who are you?" 16. Then the man with the evil spirit leaped on them, mastered them all, and so overpowered them that they fled out of the house naked and wounded.

Jesus' secrecy, however, was not restricted to hiding miracles, but extended to his teaching. It is sometimes said that he wished to avoid being regarded as a philosopher of the hellenistic type. Again the danger was real:

> Acts 17.18. Also some Epicurean and Stoic philosophers debated with him [Paul]. Some said, "What does this babbler want to say?" Others said, "He seems to be a proclaimer of foreign divinities." (This was because he was telling the good news about Jesus and the resurrection.) 19. So they took him and brought him to the Areopagus and asked him, "May we know what this new teaching is that you are presenting? 20. It sounds rather strange to us, so we would like to know what it means." 21. Now all the Athenians and the foreigners living there would spend their time in nothing but telling or hearing something new.

Still these solutions are at best only a partial explanation. They cannot account for the fact that Jesus claimed that he spoke in parables in order that he would not be understood and so that his hearers would not be forgiven (4.11f.). Even the disciples could not understand until he explained the parables. Even then, there was still much that the closest of his disciples could not understand. For instance, they did not appreciate that he could still a storm (4.35ff.). Jesus said to the disciples: "Why are you thus afraid? How is it that you have no faith?" (4.40). And though the storm had been stilled, the disciples were extremely fearful and said to one another: "Who is this man, that both the wind and the sea obey him?" (4.41). Again, the disciples did not understand when he told them to beware the yeast of the Pharisees and of Herod (8.14ff.). Even after he explained, he asked, "Do you not yet understand?" (8.21).

Even if we could precisely date Mark and set it in a particular locale, it would be impossible, I believe, to understand the nature of any standard Christian community to whom Mark was directing this particular emphasis. Two alternative explanations may be suggested.

First, Mark was written for a community that reveled in the secrecy of Jesus' teaching. We know that subsequently the Carpocratians, a Gnostic sect, liked Mark for that reason. This suggestion, I think, may be excluded. We must remember that the Gospels are a unique literary genre in antiquity: in one sense a biography, but with no sustained attempt to plot the course of the life; not an account of a man, but of a superhuman being, with the emphasis on the Passion and on the events leading up to it, and, of course, on the Resurrection. But Mark was the earliest Gospel and was used extensively and followed by Matthew and Luke. This is incomprehensible if Mark was far from the mainstream of early Christian belief.

The second suggestion is that Mark gives a tolerably accurate picture of Jesus, much as he was generally remembered. Then Jesus would be a figure of great charisma, a great worker of miracles, a great preacher who could enthrall crowds, whose teaching was enthusiastically attended, even when the reasoning was unclear. Indeed, the teaching was meant to obfuscate, and it did. Even Jesus' closest followers could not understand. They accepted the power of Jesus' message with little comprehension. The lack of clarity, the parables, were even part of the power of the message. Such religious charismatic leaders are not uncommon. The power of Jesus' message, in this view, would have disappeared shortly after his death if it had not been for belief in the Resurrection. That kept alive the power of the message and made its understanding imperative.

8

THE
SANHEDRIN

NOT ALL ASPECTS OF THE SANHEDRIN CONCERN US,
and for others only the briefest outline is required.[1] Thus, we
need not consider the Sanhedrin as a council but only as a criminal court. Nor need we know the precise number of judges who
sat for each type of crime. Several matters, though, require attention.

I

In hellenistic Israel there existed a Jewish *gerousia* from at least
the time of Antiochus the Great (223–187 B.C.).[2] The very name
of the council indicates its aristocratic nature since the term
γερουσία always denotes a nondemocratic body.[3] But by the
time Pompey the Great intervened in Jewish affairs, the composition of the gerousia had undergone change with an increase in
both the representation and power of learned men, the scribes,
who were basically Pharisees. So the court was composed of an
amalgam of the hereditary nobility, especially the chief priests

who were Sadducees, and scribes, Pharisees skilled in religious law. Pompey appointed Hyrcanus as the high priest and the leader of the nation.[4] The high priest also presided over the Sanhedrin. Gabinius, as Roman governor of Syria, divided the Jewish lands into five synedria, of which three—Jerusalem, Gazara, and Jericho—were in Judaea.[5] Thus, though in a sense the great Sanhedrin had jurisdiction over all Jews, its direct jurisdiction was restricted to part of Judaea. This situation did not last, and we learn from Josephus that a few years later its jurisdiction again stretched as far as Galilee.[6] But on Herod's death his territory was divided, and his son Archelaus succeeded only to the provinces of Judaea and Samaria. So the Sanhedrin's direct jurisdiction would be restricted to Judaea: once again it did not stretch to Galilee. This was the case in the time of Jesus when Judaea was under Roman rule and Galilee was a client state of the Romans, ruled by the tetrarch Herod Antipas.

According to Josephus,[7] Herod the Great executed all the members of the Sanhedrin at the beginning of his reign; in another account,[8] Herod executed forty-five of Antigonus's most prominent supporters. Whatever the truth may be, the effect would in either case be a great reduction in the authority of the aristocratic Sadducees. The office of chief priest was hereditary: according to the Pentateuch, only the "sons of Aaron" could sacrifice.[9] They were thus a closed class. Moreover, no one who belonged to it by legitimate birth could be excluded from it. A closed aristocratic class which does not necessarily have the strongest secular power or the support of the people and which is faced by tyrants, whether native or foreign, is always likely to be submissive: only those members who obey will have a chance to survive. The Sadducees were natural collaborators with the Romans, for example. The scribal Pharisaic members of the Sanhedrin, on the other hand, were elected, presumably on account of their learning. The important thing for us is that, as Josephus tells us, though the Sadducees were men of the highest standing, they accomplished practically nothing. They always had to give way to the Pharisees because otherwise the masses would not tolerate them.[10] There may be exaggeration here. Nonetheless, what should be stressed is that the Sadducees as the chief priests were an essential element of the Sanhedrin, especially because the high priest was its president. Without the Sadducees, the Sanhedrin could not function. For our purposes it is important to know that both Sadducees and Pharisees had essential roles to play in the Sanhedrin. We have no need, however, to try to establish who held the balance of power.[11]

II

A second issue that we must confront is whether the Sanhedrin in the time of Jesus had the power to impose a death sentence and, if so, whether it made use of the power. The answer I will give is a very strong affirmative, but the matter is controversial because of John 18.31: "Pilate said to them, 'Take him yourselves, and judge him according to your law.' The Jews replied, 'We are not permitted to put anyone to death.' " The text is unambiguous, but it is the only real evidence for the case that the Sanhedrin could not execute someone. And it is here that we must bring in the tendency of John.

As I already mentioned, I believe that John used a Pharisaic narrative tradition (that I designate S) in order to weaken it. Still, much of the original can be uncovered. The use of this Pharisaic source explains problems familiar to Johannine scholars. To begin with, John shows great knowledge of Jewish Judaean circumstances, but also makes gaffes. For instance, John

11.49–51 describes Caiaphas as high priest "that year," but high priests were appointed for life (or, more precisely, for as long as the Romans wanted). The confusion is made even worse at John 18.12–24, where both Caiaphas and his father-in-law, Annas, are referred to as the high priest.[12] The explanation of the great knowledge of Judaean Jewish circumstances on the one hand and of the howlers on the other lies in the nature of compilations. Accuracies stem from one source, the mistakes from another.[13] But who is responsible for the mistakes? The answer must be that at least the redactor, the evangelist himself, is responsible. It is he who has the final say. Thus, what is correct may go back to an earlier source; what is wrong must show the ignorance of the redactor if of no one else. We must believe that the redactor knew little of Jewish customs as they were in Israel before the destruction of the Temple in A.D. 70.

It is the nature of compilations that also explains another noted feature of John: on the one hand it shows remarkable sympathy for Jews, yet it is the most virulently anti-Jewish Gospel. The sympathy comes from the Pharisaic source used in John; the anti-Jewish sentiment is that of the redactor himself.[14]

I do not at this stage want to claim that John 18.31 is inaccurate. Rather, I want to set it aside temporarily, in order to see what the other evidence looks like in its absence. The problem for us is that the text is so clear that it is difficult not to read the other texts in light of it. But if we accept the possibility that John could be wildly inaccurate, then the other texts may perhaps be read more naturally. If they do point decisively in another direction, then we must address the issue of John's accuracy.[15]

The first evidence that the Sanhedrin could impose the death penalty is the Mishnah tractate, Sanhedrin, which for instance sets out in detail those offenses punishable by death,[16] aspects of procedure,[17] evidence,[18] modes of execution,[19] the offenses for which each mode is appropriate,[20] and the nature of the crimes.[21] One passage may serve as an illustration:

Mishnah Sanhedrin 6.1. When sentence [of stoning] has been passed they take him forth to stone him. The place of stoning was outside [far away from] the court, as it is written, *Bring forth him that hath cursed without the camp.*[22] One man stands at the door of the court with a towel in his hand, and another, mounted on a horse, far away from him [but near enough] to see him. If [in the court] one said, "I have somewhat to argue in favour of his acquittal," that man waves the towel and the horse runs and stops him [that was going forth to be stoned]. Even if he himself said, "I have somewhat to argue in favour of my acquittal," they must bring him back, be it four times or five, provided that there is aught of substance in his words. If then they found him innocent they set him free; otherwise he goes forth to be stoned. A herald goes out before him [calling], "Such-a-one, the son of such-a-one, is going forth to be stoned for that he committed such or such an offense. Such-a-one and such-a-one are witnesses against him. If any man knoweth aught in favour of his acquittal let him come and plead it." 2. When he was about ten cubits from the place of stoning they used to say to him, "Make thy confession," for such is the way of them that have been condemned to death to make confession, for every one that makes his confession has a share in the world to come. For so have we found it with Achan. Joshua said to him, *My son, give, I pray thee, glory to the Lord, the God of Israel, and make confession unto him, and tell me now what thou has done; hide it not from me. And Achan answered Joshua and said, Of a truth I have sinned against the Lord, the God of Israel, and thus and thus have I done.*[23] Whence do we learn that his confession made atonement for him? It is written, *And Joshua said, Why hast thou troubled us? The Lord shall trouble thee this day*[24]— *this day* thou shalt be troubled, but in the world to come thou shalt not be troubled. If he knows not how to make his confession they say to him, "Say, May my death be an atonement for all my sins." R. Judah says: If he knew that he was condemned because of false testimony he should say, "Let my death be an atonement for all my sins excepting this sin." They said to him: If so, every one would speak after this fashion to show his innocence.

3. When he was four cubits from the place of stoning they stripped off his clothes. A man is kept covered in front and a woman both in front and behind. So R. Judah. But the Sages say: A man is stoned naked but a woman is not stoned naked.

4. The place of stoning was twice the height of a man. One of the witnesses knocked him down on his loins; if he turned over on his heart the witness turned him over again on his loins. If he straightway died that sufficed; but if not, the second [witness] took the stone and dropped it on his heart. If he straightway died, that sufficed; but if not, he was stoned by all Israel, for it is written, *The hand of the witnesses shall be first upon him to put him to death and afterward the hand of all the people.*[25] All that have been stoned must be hanged. So R. Eliezer. But the Sages say: None is hanged save the blasphemer and the idolater. A man is hanged with his face to the people and a woman with her face towards the gallows. So R. Eliezer. But the Sages say: A man is hanged but a woman is not hanged. R. Eliezer said to them: Did not Simeon ben Shetah hang women

in Ashkelon? They answered: He hanged eighty women, whereas two ought not to be judged in the one day. How did they hang a man? They put a beam into the ground and a piece of wood jutted from it. The two hands [of the body] were brought together and [in this fashion] it was hanged. R. Jose says: The beam was made to lean against a wall and one hanged the corpse thereon as the butchers do. And they let it down at once: if it remained there overnight a negative command is thereby transgressed, for it is written, *His body shall not remain all night upon the tree, but thou shalt surely bury him the same day; for he that is hanged is a curse against God;*[26] as if to say: Why was this one hanged? Because he blessed the Name, and the Name of Heaven was found profaned.

The issue for us is thus not whether the Sanhedrin ever had the right to impose the death penalty, but whether that right which existed was taken away when Judaea was ruled by Roman procurators. The answer is that the right was not taken away. First, there is not the slightest evidence that it was, before the destruction of the Temple and Jerusalem. Second, there was no reason for the Romans to deprive the Sanhedrin of that right: the Romans would have exclusive right to try secular capital cases; the Sanhedrin the exclusive right to try Jews for religious capital cases not involving a Roman criminal offense. Third, the Romans were extremely tolerant of Jewish religious practices and would be most unlikely to deprive the highest religious court of its supreme authority. Fourth, the Roman practice was to leave as much administration as possible in the hands of the locals.[27]

A second piece of evidence is in Philo's *Embassy to Gaius*. Philo is reporting the embassy that complained in A.D. 39 or 40 to the emperor Gaius (better known as Caligula) about the proposal to install a colossal statue in the sanctuary in the innermost part of the Temple:

> 307. And if any priest, to say nothing of the other Jews, and not merely one of the lowest priests but of those who are ranked directly below the chief, goes in either by himself or with the high priest, and further even if the high priest enters on two days in the year or thrice or four times on the same day, death without appeal is his doom. So greatly careful was the law-giver to guard the inmost sanctuary, the one and only place which he wished to keep preserved untrodden and untouched.

Thus, by law any Jew, any priest, who entered the sanctuary would be executed. Even the high priest would suffer that fate if he entered the sanctuary except on the permitted occasions. The text stresses that this was the law at the time of the embassy. We are not told which body enforced the law, but it could be none other than the Sanhedrin. At the time of the embassy, which is not long after the death of Jesus, Judaea was certainly governed by a Roman procurator.

Philo provides us with even more evidence:

> *Embassy to Gaius* 212: Still more abounding and peculiar is the zeal of them for the temple, and the strongest proof of this is that death without appeal is the sentence against those of other races who penetrate into its inner confines. For the outer are open to everyone wherever they come from.

Philo writes in the present tense of a rule then existing, also in the context of the embassy to Gaius. And for this offense the court could put even non-Jews to death. Philo's report is more than confirmed by Josephus:

> *Jewish War* 6.124: Titus, yet more deeply distressed, again upbraided John and his friends. "Was it not you," he said, "most abominable wretches, who placed this balustrade before your sanctuary? Was it not you that ranged along it those slabs, engraved in Greek characters and in our own, proclaiming that none may pass the barrier? And did we not permit you to put to death any who passed it, even were he a Roman?"[28]

In A.D. 70 the Romans were besieging the Jews in the Temple, and the general Titus is here expressing reluctance to destroy it. He declares that the Romans permitted the Jews to put to death even Roman citizens who entered the Temple sanctuary. If the Sanhedrin could execute Romans even for one crime, it must have had capital jurisdiction over Jews. Pace Raymond E. Brown, it is not significant for Roman control over the Sanhedrin's power to impose the death penalty that these notices were set up with Roman permission.[29] The point of the Roman permission is to allow the Sanhedrin in this exceptional case to exert authority, even impose death, on non-Jews, even Roman citizens, as well as on Jews. The Romans could have little interest in whether the Sanhedrin executed Jews for religious crimes.

Josephus provides further proof of the Sanhedrin executing capital punishment:

> *Jewish Antiquities* 20.199. The younger Ananus, who, as we have said, had been appointed to the High Priesthood, was rash in his temper and unusually daring. He followed the school of the Sadducees, who are indeed more heartless than any of the other Jews, as I have already explained,

when they sit in judgment. 200. Possessed of such a character, Ananus thought that he had a favourable opportunity because Festus was dead and Albinus was still on the way. And so he convened the judges of the Sanhedrin and brought before them a man named James, the brother of Jesus who was called the Christ, and certain others. He accused them of having transgressed the law and delivered them up to be stoned. 201. Those of the inhabitants of the city who were considered the most fair-minded and who were strict in observance of the law were offended at this. They therefore secretly sent to King Agrippa urging him, for Ananus had not even been correct in his first step, to order him to desist from any further such actions. 202. Certain of them even went to meet Albinus, who was on his way from Alexandria, and informed him that Ananus had no authority to convene the Sanhedrin without his consent. Convinced by these words, Albinus angrily wrote to Ananus threatening to take vengeance upon him. 203. King Agrippa, because of Ananus's action, deposed him from the high priesthood which he had held for three months and replaced him with Jesus the son of Damnaeus.

Here we have explicit testimony of the Sanhedrin condemning to death by stoning, though the offense is not precisely specified. James, the brother of Jesus, had become the Christian leader. Few have considered this passage interpolated, in contrast to the standard attitude to the passage in Josephus that discusses Jesus.[30] That Ananus II had behaved wrongfully does not affect the importance of the testimony. The Roman procurator Festus had died, his replacement Albinus was on his way, and Ananus convened the Sanhedrin. His offense, and that of his fellow judges, was not in killing James: that would be murder if the

Sanhedrin had no power to execute. Rather, he should have had the consent of the Roman procurator before he summoned the council as is even spelled out at the end of § 202.[31] His offense was in summoning the Sanhedrin without obtaining the consent of the procurator. This conclusion will be important to us in another context. If as seems likely—though we have no evidence—the high priest usually wore the sacred vestments when he presided over the Sanhedrin, we have an explanation of the political purpose of the Romans keeping control of the vestments.[32] They thus would have foreknowledge of any meeting of the Sanhedrin. But the issue must not be pressed because at least on this occasion the high priest was not so clothed. Again, we have the testimony of St. Paul:

> Acts 26.9. "Indeed, I myself was convinced that I ought to do many things against the name of Jesus of Nazareth. 10. And that is what I did in Jerusalem: with authority received from the chief priests, I not only locked up many of the saints in prison, but I also cast my vote against them when they were being condemned to death.

Paul was a self-confessed Pharisee (Acts 26.5). He is here assuredly speaking of the condemnation to death of Christians not by a Roman but by a Jewish authority. That he is discussing formal proceedings before an assembly is shown by his speaking of his vote in favor of death. This assembly can be nothing other than the Sanhedrin, which again is shown as having the power to impose the death penalty.

The evidence in Acts regarding the stoning of Stephen is perhaps by itself not quite so conclusive. Stephen was accused of blasphemy and brought before the Sanhedrin (Acts 6.11–15). Stephen preached a sermon in effect, explaining his stance. Then, at a certain point:

Acts 7.54. When they heard these things, they became enraged and ground their teeth at Stephen. 55. But filled with the Holy Spirit, he gazed into heaven and saw the glory of God and Jesus standing at the right hand of God. 56. "Look," he said, "I see the heavens opened and the Son of man standing at the right hand of God!" 57. But they covered their ears, and with a loud shout all rushed together against him. 58. Then they dragged him out of the city and began to stone him; and the witnesses laid their coats at the feet of a young man named Saul. 59. While they were stoning Stephen, he prayed, "Lord Jesus, receive my spirit." 60. Then he knelt down and cried out in a loud voice, "Lord, do not hold this sin against them." When he had said this, he died.

There is no doubt that the narrative recounts a trial before the Sanhedrin, and the charge seems to be blasphemy. Those who covered their ears and rushed upon Stephen were the judges: the public would not be present in the council chamber. They dragged him out of the city, in accordance with Mishnah Sanhedrin 6.1. And they stoned Stephen. But there is an element of lynching. The judges should not have pronounced sentence on the day of the trial. After a verdict of guilty, the judges should have reconvened the following morning to reconsider their verdict and to pass sentence:

> Mishnah Sanhedrin 5.5. If they found him innocent they set him free; otherwise they leave his sentence over until the morrow. [In the meantime] they went together in pairs, they ate a little (but they used to drink no wine the whole day), and they discussed the matter all night, and early on the morrow they came to the court. He that favored acquittal says: "I declared him innocent [yesterday] and I still

declare him innocent"; and he that favored conviction says, "I declared him guilty [yesterday] and I still declare him guilty." He that had favored conviction may now acquit, but he that had favored acquittal may not retract and favour conviction.

There are two possibilities. Either we say the Sanhedrin convicted Stephen of blasphemy, which was a crime they could punish by stoning, and in anger they stoned him prematurely; or we say the Sanhedrin convicted Stephen of blasphemy, which was a crime they could no longer punish by death by stoning, but in anger they lynched him by stoning.[33] I favor the first, but really because I accept from other evidence that the Sanhedrin could impose the death penalty. A final piece of evidence is in the third-century letter of Origen to Africanus:

14. But you say, "How could they who were in captivity pass sentence of death?" asserting, I know not on what grounds, that Susanna was the wife of a king, because of the name Joakim. The answer is, that it is no uncommon thing, when great nations become subject, that the king should allow the captives to use their own laws and courts of justice. Now, for instance, that the Romans rule, and the Jews pay the half-shekel to them, how great power by the concession of Caesar the ethnarch has; so that we, who have had experience of it, know that he differs in little from a true king! Private trials are held according to the law, and some are condemned to death. And though there is not full license for this, still it is not done without the knowledge of the ruler, as we learned and were convinced of when we spent much time in the country of that people. And yet the Romans only take account of two tribes, while at that time besides Judah there were the ten tribes of Israel.

Probably the Assyrians contented themselves with holding them in subjection, and conceded to them their own judicial processes.

Africanus had written to Origen, claiming that the story of Susanna in the Book of Daniel was a recent forgery. Origen now replies. The part that interests us is his statement that conquerors commonly allow the vanquished to use their own courts and laws—that the Jews under Roman rule do hold private trials according to law and do condemn some people to death. He says that though they have not full license to do this, the Romans are aware of what goes on. He vouches for this from private experience. Origen was in Palestine for some time from 215 after the massacre of Christians at Alexandria. If Jews were still sentencing to death at that time under Roman rule, they certainly were doing so in the lifetime of Jesus when the Sanhedrin flourished.[34]

We must now return to John 18.31, which contrary to all the other evidence declares that the Jews could not execute anyone.[35] Not only is the weight of evidence conclusive against the accuracy of the text, but I have shown (I believe) that the evangelist was unfamiliar with basic facts of Judaean Judaism. But there is more against the accuracy of the text. From the text itself we see that Pilate was unaware that the Sanhedrin could not condemn to death: "Take him yourselves, and judge him according to your law." Moreover, the claim that the Jews could not put someone to death did not persuade Pilate. When the crowd insisted on crucifixion despite the fact that he had found no case against Jesus, he said: "Take him yourselves and crucify him: I find no case against him" (John 19.6). How could Pilate say this if the Sanhedrin had no power to impose a death sentence?

It is enough for present purposes, I believe, to show that the claim in John 18.31 cannot stand against the overwhelming evidence that the Sanhedrin in the time of Jesus had the power to impose and inflict the death sentence, that Pilate's words in the very same context appear to deny the claim, and that in other regards John betrays ignorance of Judaean Judaism in the procuratorial period. Still, I should like to explain the background to John's error.

In contrast to the Synoptics, John has Romans involved in the arrest of Jesus (John 18.12). The Jews are shown as thoroughly justified in wanting Jesus' death: if he lives, the Romans will destroy the nation and the Temple (John 11.47ff.). The Jewish leaders do not try Jesus for a religious offense; instead, they hand him over to the Romans as a criminal (John 18.28ff.). The evangelist is hostile to the Pharisaic tradition responsible for this, but it is so well established that he cannot ignore it; instead, he makes small but subtle changes to defang it and change its message. Hence, the evangelist is responsible for the line "We are not permitted to put anyone to death." The point is that the Sanhedrin has not sentenced Jesus to death, but for John the evangelist this is only because it was not allowed to execute him. Here as in other instances the evangelist is ignorant of circumstances in Israel before the destruction of the Temple.

III

A further issue is whether the trial before the Sanhedrin was legal. A first question as to whether a trial could lawfully be held in a private house may quickly be set aside because an answer is not really needed. There is a great deal of evidence that the Sanhedrin had a special meeting place,[36] even if there is doubt as to where that was.[37] But there is no conclusive proof that a trial held elsewhere was unlawful on that account, unless one holds, as seems reasonable, that Mishnah Sanhedrin 11.2 implies that a meeting could only be held in one of the places mentioned there.

On the other hand, in Mark (14.53ff.) and Matthew (26.57ff.) the trial before the Sanhedrin was held at night and a capital trial at night was illegal:

> Mishnah Sanhedrin 4.1. In noncapital cases they hold the trial during the daytime and the verdict may be reached during the night; in capital cases they hold the trial during the daytime and the verdict also must be reached during the daytime. In noncapital cases the verdict, whether of acquittal or of conviction, may be reached the same day; in capital cases a verdict of acquittal may be reached on the same day, but a verdict of conviction not until the following day.

There are further minor indications of illegality if the law stated in the Mishnah existed in Jesus' time.[38]

IV

A further aspect of the Sanhedrin to be touched upon is the evidentiary requirements for conviction. The main authority is the Mishnah Sanhedrin:

> 5.1. They used to prove witnesses with seven inquiries: In what week of years? In what year? In what month? On what date in the month? On what day? In what hour? In what place? (R. Jose says: [They asked only,] On what day? In what hour? In what place?) [Moreover they asked:] Do ye recognize him? Did ye warn him? If a man had committed idolatry [they asked the witnesses], What did he worship? and, How did he worship it?
>
> 2. The more a judge tests the evidence the more is he

deserving of praise: Ben Zakkai once tested the evidence even to the inquiring about the stalks of figs. Wherein do the inquiries differ from the cross-examination? If to the inquiries one [of the two witnesses] answered, "I do not know," their evidence becomes invalid; but if to the cross-examination one answered, "I do not know," or if they both answered, "We do not know," their evidence remains valid. Yet if they contradict one another, whether during the inquiries or the cross-examination, their evidence becomes invalid.

3. If one said, "On the second of the month," and the other said, "On the third," their evidence remains valid, since one may have known that the month was intercalated and the other did not know that the month was intercalated; but if one said, "On the third," and the other said, "On the fifth," their evidence becomes invalid. If one said, "At the second hour," and the other said, "At the third," their evidence remains valid; but if one said, "At the third hour," and the other said, "At the fifth," their evidence becomes invalid. R. Judah says: It remains valid; but if one said, "At the fifth hour," and the other said, "At the seventh," their evidence becomes invalid since at the fifth hour the sun is in the east and at the seventh it is in the west.

4. They afterward brought in the second witness and proved him. If their words were found to agree together they begin [to examine the evidence] in favour of acquittal. If one of the witnesses said, "I have somewhat to argue in favour of his acquittal," or if one of the disciples said, "I have somewhat to argue in favour of his conviction," they silence him. If one of the disciples said, "I have somewhat to argue in favour of his acquittal," they bring him up and set him among them and he does not come down from thence the whole day. If there is aught of substance in his words

they listen to him. Even if the accused said, "I have somewhat to argue in favour of my acquittal," they listen to him, provided that there is aught of substance in his words.

Thus, the requirements were very strict. For proof by eyewitnesses, two witnesses were required. They were examined separately—the purpose of this is seen in the book of Susanna—and their testimony had to agree in every particular.[39]

V

The last issue we should address is the nature of the crime with which Jesus was charged.[40] At Mark 14.64, after Jesus had admitted to being the Messiah, the high priest said " ἠκούσατε τῆς βλασφημίας" "You have heard his blasphemy." In Matthew 26.65, the word is " ἐβλασφήμησεν," "he blasphemed." Much earlier, he was also regarded as blaspheming. Thus, when he said to the paralyzed man that his sins were forgiven, the scribes who were present thought he blasphemed (Mark 2.5ff.). No other charge at the trial of Jesus is mentioned, but there is a problem: according to the (admittedly later) Mishnah in tractate Sanhedrin 7.5, blasphemy is solely committed by uttering the name of God. And the Greek words that give rise to our words to blaspheme and blasphemy have wider meanings than our words. They may refer not only to insults to a deity but also to ordinary defamation or insult.[41]

Still, it is most probable that blasphemy was the charge. The death that Jesus expected was by stoning (Matthew 23.37; Luke 13.34), and this was the penalty established for particular crimes, including blasphemy:

Mishnah Sanhedrin 7.4. These are they that are to be stoned: he that has connexion with his mother, his father's wife, his daughter-in-law, a male, or a beast, and the woman that suffers connexion with a beast, and the blasphemer and the idolator, and he that offers any of his seed to Molech, and he that has a familiar spirit and the soothsayer, and he that profanes the Sabbath, and he that curses his father or his mother, and he that has connexion with a girl that is betrothed, and he that beguiles [others to idolatry], and he that leads [a whole town] astray, and the sorcerer and a stubborn and rebellious son.

None of these other crimes for which stoning was the accepted penalty would seem to be appropriate except perhaps leading a town astray, but even that is closely connected with blasphemy. Second, only blasphemy is mentioned in the context of the trial, so it should be presumed that this was in fact the charge. Third, it is as the reason for conviction that Mark and Matthew have the high priest say (in Greek) that Jesus blasphemed; it is most unlikely that the tradition behind the Gospels should report him using that terminology untechnically. Fourth, the Jewish leaders are represented as certainly seeking to put Jesus to death, but no other charge entailing the death penalty, no matter how inflicted, seems as relevant.

We should hold that in this, as in other regards, the Mishnah, as is generally agreed,[42] did not set forth the legal system of the Sanhedrin as it was before A.D. 70, but as an ideal. Certainly, the Sanhedrin was not at that time a council of scholars as represented in the Mishnah but was composed of an amalgam of hereditary members and scholars, as it appears in the Gospels and Josephus.[43]

My point in the last paragraph should be clarified. What I would emphatically not accept is that, in representing the legal system as an ideal, the rules in the Mishnah had no contact with reality as it existed before A.D. 70. That is, while we cannot always accept the rules in the Mishnah at face value for the period before the destruction of the Temple, we cannot discount them as intellectual fantasy. It is inconceivable to me that scholars, to no apparent purpose, would debate at enormous length legal and religious rules that they themselves had fabricated. For example, if the Mishnah sets out various forms of capital punishment, describes the crimes for which each is appropriate, and postulates the requirements for each separate offense, then it strains my credulity to suggest there is no basis for this. In any event, law is a discipline that generally is slow to develop and slow to change. As a basic proposition we can say that the law of today rests not only on the law of yesterday but on that of hundreds of years ago. To some extent an analogy may be drawn from the *Digest* of the emperor Justinian. This was published in 533 as law for the Byzantine empire and is composed of juristic texts from the Roman empire; almost none of the texts is from later than 235. Of course, the Byzantines were careful in what they selected and, of course, modern scholars dispute the extent to which the texts were changed, but still it would be agreed that in the main the texts give the substance of law as it was three hundred years before. So, I suggest, it is with the Mishnah. Much may be idealized of law and of the Sanhedrin as it was before A.D. 70, but much of the actuality remains.[44]

Indeed, there is evidence from Jewish writings in Greek that in the first centuries B.C. and A.D. blasphemy meant more than uttering or cursing the name of God, and that βλασφημία and βλασφημέω were the appropriate terms. Thus, 1 Maccabees 2.6 records: "He saw the blasphemies (βλασφημίας) being committed in Judah and Jerusalem." 1 Maccabees was originally in Hebrew, but it has survived only in Greek and Latin manuscripts and was probably written shortly after the death of John Hyrcanus in 104 B.C.[45] As the verses that follow show, it concerns the defilement of the Temple by Antiochus IV. More than that, the verse says, "He saw ($\varepsilon\tilde{\iota}\delta\varepsilon\nu$) the blasphemies," and a verb of seeing would not be appropriate for an offense that consisted solely of speech.[46]

If we can accept that the trial of Jesus was on the charge of blasphemy, then conviction at the first hearing in Mark followed on the admission that he was the Messiah. The only evidence we know of what was adduced for any crime was that he had said he would tear down the Temple and rebuild it in three days. And we know of an earlier suspicion of blasphemy when he said, "Your sins are forgiven."[47]

9

✝

PONTIUS
PILATE

✝ ✝ ✝

SCHOLARS ARE OFTEN TROUBLED BY WHAT THEY RE-
gard as contradictory depictions of Pontius Pilate in Josephus
and the Gospels.[1] In Josephus, Pilate appears arrogant, stubborn,
cruel, wrong-headed, and contemptuous of Jewish religious sen-
sibilities. Scholars see the Pontius Pilate of the Gospels as weak,
one who caves in to the Jewish leaders, and who against his own
wishes condemns to death a man whom he knows to be innocent.[2] Naturally, it is this second picture that is widely thought
to be inaccurate. I agree, but only because I believe it to be a
misunderstanding of what is going on in the Gospels.

According to Josephus, Pontius Pilate was sent as procurator to
Judaea in A.D. 26. Secretly at night he introduced the legionary
standards into Jerusalem, something that his predecessors had
not done. When the presence of the standards was discovered
at daybreak, it caused great upset among the Jews. The standards, unlike those of his predecessors, contained medallions of
the emperor, and thus were considered offensive because of the
Jewish prohibition against graven images.[3] The Jews believed

their law was being trampled underfoot because they allowed no image to be in the city.[4] Country people flocked to Jerusalem. Pilate was in Caesarea. The people crowded there and begged him to remove the standards from Jerusalem and to uphold their laws. Pilate refused, so the people lay down around his home and remained that way for five days. On the sixth day, Pilate summoned the crowd before his tribunal, as if he would answer their complaints. Instead, he gave a signal for his armed soldiers to surround the crowd. Pilate threatened to cut them down if they did not accept the images of Caesar, and he ordered the soldiers to draw their swords. The Jews threw themselves on the ground, stretched out their throats, and cried that they would die rather than break the law. In astonishment at their religious zeal, Pilate ordered the immediate removal of the standards from Jerusalem.

Subsequently Pilate caused a new uproar when he used the holy treasure known as Corbonas to build an aqueduct.[5] Corban was a gift to God,[6] and Josephus links it with a payment made in order to be freed from a vow.[7] It should not have been used by a Gentile for secular purposes, no matter how worthy. The crowd gathered around Pilate's tribunal—he was in Jerusalem at the time—but he had foreseen this, and he had placed soldiers among the crowd, in disguise and with orders not to use their swords but to beat rioters with sticks. Many Jews were killed by the blows or by being crushed by the fleeing mob. Josephus also gives a rather different version in his *Jewish Antiquities* 18.59: the Jews, caught unaware, were not afraid, and no mention is made of those trampled underfoot.

Pilate's character is also indicated in his treatment of the Samaritans. A rogue persuaded them to go to Mount Gerizim, their holiest place, where he would show them, he said, the sacred vessels that Moses had placed there. A great crowd of

Samaritans armed themselves and went to a village called Tirathana from which they hoped to climb Mount Gerizim. But Pilate blocked their route with cavalry and heavily armed infantry who killed some Samaritans while others fled. Of the many prisoners, Pilate put to death the leaders and the most influential. In consequence, a council of the Samaritans went to Vitellius, the Roman governor of Syria, and charged Pilate with the slaughter.[8] They claimed they had met in Tirathana, not as rebels against the Romans but as refugees from Pilate's persecution. Vitellius ordered Pilate to return to Rome to account to Tiberius for his actions, but Tiberius had died before Pilate arrived. All in all, for Josephus Pilate was a harsh and tactless procurator and not very successful. Josephus's picture is supported by Philo, who, perhaps with exaggeration, describes Pilate as stubborn and inflexible, a blend of self-will and relentlessness.[9]

One verse of Luke, 13.1, should also be noted in the context of Pilate's savagery: "At that very time there were some present who told him about the Galileans whose blood Pilate had mingled with their sacrifices." Since Jews could sacrifice only at the Temple in Jerusalem,[10] any such slaughter must have taken place there. But we know nothing more about the event.

To understand the behavior of Pontius Pilate at the trial of Jesus in the Gospels, we should look at the issues from his perspective. And for the reasons already discussed, we should take Mark as the basic text.

The chief priests brought Jesus to Pilate in chains (Mark 15.1): "Pilate asked, 'Are you the King of the Jews?' and Jesus answered, 'You say so'" (Mark 15.2). Pilate clearly had some knowledge of what was going on. He could scarcely have been so out of touch as to be unaware of the triumphal welcome of Jesus on his way to Jerusalem. He also must have known of the outrage of the cleansing of the Temple because the main Ro man military tower, the Antonia, was adjacent to the Temple. (And, surely, the Romans would have had informers?) Moreover, there must have been continual and close contact between Caiaphas and Pilate. The office of high priest was in actuality at the will of the Romans, and Caiaphas held it from A.D. 18 to 36, an exceptionally long time.[11] Also, in Mark, it was Pilate who took the initiative. Only after Pilate asked Jesus if he were the king of the Jews did the chief priests accuse Jesus (Mark 15.3). In addition, as we saw with regard to the execution of James by order of the Sanhedrin, the high priest was punished because he summoned the Sanhedrin without obtaining the consent of the Roman procurator.[12] In all probability, among the reasons for the Romans controlling the vestments of the high priest was the desire to know when the Sanhedrin was going to meet.[13]

Mark 15.3f. makes it plain that the priests came with accusations, not with a conviction. They made many charges, but the final conviction was not for a religious offense but for sedition, because Jesus had claimed to be the king of the Jews (Mark 15.26). Jesus made no answer to Pilate's further interrogation, and Pilate was amazed (Mark 15.4f.). It was presumably at this point that Jesus was convicted by the Roman procurator. Refusal to answer would be a sufficient sign of obduracy. The rest of the proceedings are based on the idea that Jesus had been convicted, and the narrative presents no other point where a guilty verdict would seem more plausible. But thereafter Pilate made strong efforts to release Jesus.

The Sanhedrin wanted Jesus put to death, but they had finally failed to convict him. We may presume from Mark 14.56ff. that the crux was that members of the court believed that the strict rabbinic standards of proof had not been met. Some judges might also have been shocked by the illegality of meeting at night or feared the wrath of the crowd. So they wanted Pilate to do the dirty work. But why should he? On the one hand, he had no technical difficulty in finding a guilty verdict. And there can be no doubt that the Roman procurator (or whatever title he had) of Judaea had the right to put a noncitizen to death without an appeal.[14] But to execute Jesus would be to do the bidding of the Sanhedrin, and it would expose the Romans to the dangers of the very riots that the Sanhedrin feared. So he tested out the feelings of the crowd, and only when he was satisfied that they favored the execution did he hand over Jesus for execution. On the other hand, Pilate was aware that Jesus had caused trouble and that if he were released he might cause more. Pilate had no reason not to execute him once he was sure that this would please the crowd. In the narrative there is no indication that Pilate had any pity for Jesus. Squeamishness over executions lightly carried out was not a noted characteristic of Roman public officials.

Mark 15.6 relates that Pilate had a custom at the festival of releasing a prisoner for the Jews, whomsoever they wanted. The existence of any such custom is inherently improbable. It is not evidenced for any other province or, within Judea, for any other procurator. Such sensitivity does not fit any view of Pilate's character. In a province so troubled by revolutionaries, such a custom would also have been extremely unwise. In addition, the festival was over. Moreover, Pilate did not follow what is said to have been his custom, of releasing to them whomsoever they wanted. Instead, he asked if they wanted him to release to them the king of the Jews. The crowd insisted that Jesus be crucified and asked for Barabbas to be released.

Pilate had no such custom, I suggest, but it must be accounted for.[15] I propose the following hypothesis: Pilate was unwilling to face the possibilities of rioting if he executed Jesus. So he said something like, "Because of the festival I will release a prisoner for you. Do you want me to release the King of the Jews?" This was not a custom and was not intended to start one, but as a result of the supposed wording "Because of the festival," it came to be thought of as one in the Markan tradition. When the crowd shouted out in favor of Barabbas, Pilate no longer had any reason to save Jesus. The danger he had feared did not exist.

The same alleged custom appears in Matthew 27.15ff., which is dependent on Mark, to much the same purpose, though here Pilate's wife intervenes futilely to save Jesus. The account in Luke is again different. Pilate, on learning that Jesus is a Galilean, does not condemn him but sends him to Herod Antipas in Jerusalem (Luke 23.6ff.). Herod eventually sends him back to Pilate, who summons the chief priests, the leaders, and the people and tells them that neither he nor Herod has found Jesus guilty and that he intends to release him after a flogging. But the crowd insists that he release Barabbas and crucify Jesus, and Pilate does.

The account in Luke is very unlikely even if we accept verse 17, "Now he was obliged to release someone for them at the festival," which is generally regarded as a later insertion in some manuscripts. To begin with, Pilate has just declared Jesus not guilty. He would be very weak indeed if he now executed Jesus because that was the whim of the crowd. Then again, the Sanhedrin had just declared Jesus guilty (Luke 22.66), even though the proceedings were illegal. They should have carried out the execution themselves, and Pilate should not have been involved.

The account in John is again different and again implausible:

> John 18.38. Pilate asked him, "What is truth?" After he had said this, he went out to the Jews again and told them, "I find no case against him. 39. But you have a custom that I release someone for you at the Passover. Do you want me

to release for you the King of the Jews?" 40. They shouted in reply, "Not this man, but Barabbas!" Now Barabbas was a bandit.

This time the custom is said to be Jewish. But if it were, it would not have been restricted to Pilate's procuratorship (and we have no other evidence for its existence), and the Jews would not have needed to be reminded of it. Nor is it likely that Pilate, after stating that he had found no case against Jesus, would proceed to his execution.

The ease with which a custom comes to be regarded as established must be stressed.[16] To settle custom as law, one court decision may be regarded as demonstrating "the custom." On an anecdotal level: I held a drinks party for my students in two consecutive semesters. Because of weather conditions I held the fall party at the beginning of the semester, the spring party near the end. In my spring student evaluations it was suggested I should hold my cocktail party near the beginning of the semester so that students could get to know me sooner. Two parties thus made a custom; the only outstanding issue was timing, yet the students in the two semesters were different people. Pilate offered once to release a prisoner *for the festival:* that—because of the stated reason—was treated as establishing a custom. This helps to explain why there were doubts over whose custom it was and the parameters of the supposed custom.

For the Crucifixion, the hostility of the crowd to Jesus is pivotal. If the people had clamored for Jesus' freedom Pilate would have released him. But why was the crowd so hostile after its enthusiastic welcome as Jesus approached Jerusalem? There are, I suggest, a number of factors. First, the crowd need not have been composed of the same people. Those who had no enthusiasm for Jesus and his miracles would not have turned up in numbers to welcome him. Second, the so-called cleansing of the Temple itself must have been very offensive to many ordinary observing Jews. And Jesus did nothing thereafter to redeem himself in their eyes: he performed no more miracles. Third, the trick question whether it was lawful to pay the tax to the Romans may have had the impact the Pharisees wanted. Jesus would have seemed to be an appeaser, not interested in driving out the Romans, and above all not the Messiah. Fourth, the very fact that Jesus was now a prisoner could have caused people to lose faith in him. Last, the crowd could have been turned against Jesus as a result of the incitement of the chief priests (Mark 15.11; Matthew 27.20, which adds the elders). The fickleness of the crowd is a stock theme in history. Dionysius of Halicarnassus makes Licinius Stolo declare "that there is no wild beast more bloodthirsty than the populace, which does not spare even those who feed it." [17]

The nature of the prisoner released to the Jews cannot be clearly established, whether his name was Barabbas, "son of Abbas" or Barrabbas, "son of the teacher." [18] We should probably accept that he was a historical person, but little more is known. Mark 15.7 says he was bound with the rebels who had committed murder in the rebellion. The text does not say that Barabbas had committed murder or was necessarily a revolutionary. John 18.40 describes Barabbas as a λῃστής, which is a standard word for brigand but which is used by Josephus with the sense of "Zealot." [19]

But if Pilate gave way to the Sanhedrin and executed Jesus rather than insist that they do so, he took his revenge. On the cross he set the offensive inscription, "The King of the Jews." [20] The offensiveness is well brought out in John even if we doubt the historical veracity of his detailed account:

John 19.19. Pilate also had an inscription written and put on the cross. It read, "Jesus of Nazareth, the King of the Jews." 20. Many of the Jews read this inscription, because the place where Jesus was crucified was near the city; and it was written in Hebrew, in Latin, and in Greek. 21. Then the chief priests of the Jews said to Pilate, "Do not write, 'The King of the Jews.' but 'this man said, I am King of the Jews.' " 22. Pilate answered, "What I have written I have written."

10

✝

THE
SLAVONIC
JOSEPHUS

✝ ✝ ✝

TO THIS POINT I HAVE AVOIDED DEALING WITH THE
famous, but largely ignored, passage about Jesus' ministry and
crucifixion that appears in the Slavonic version of Josephus's
Jewish War but that is absent from the Greek manuscripts:[1]

> It was at that time that a man appeared—if "man" is
> the right word—who had all the attributes of a man but
> seemed to be something greater. His actions, certainly, were
> superhuman, for he worked such wonderful and amazing
> miracles that I for one cannot regard him as a man; yet in
> view of his likeness to ourselves I cannot regard him as an
> angel either. Everything that some hidden power enabled
> him to do he did by an authoritative word. Some people said
> that their first lawgiver had risen from the dead and had
> effected many marvelous cures; others thought he was a
> messenger from heaven. However, in many ways he broke
> the law—for instance, he did not observe the Sabbath in

the traditional manner. At the same time his conduct was above reproach. He did not need to use his hands: a word sufficed to fulfill his every purpose.

Many of the common people flocked after him and followed his teaching. There was a wave of excited expectation that he would enable the Jewish tribes to throw off the Roman yoke. As a rule he was to be found opposite the City on the Mount of Olives, where also he healed the sick. He gathered round him 150 assistants and masses of followers. When they saw his ability to do whatever he wished by a word, they told him that they wanted him to enter the City, destroy the Roman troops, and make himself king; but he took no notice.

When the suggestion came to the ears of the Jewish authorities, they met under the chairmanship of the high priest and exclaimed: "We are utterly incapable of resisting the Romans; but as the blow is about to fall we'd better go and tell Pilate what we've heard, and steer clear of trouble, in case he gets to know from someone else and confiscates our property, puts us to death, and turns our children adrift." So they went and told Pilate, who sent troops and butchered many of the common people. He then had the Miracle-worker brought before him, held an inquiry, and expressed the opinion that he was a benefactor, not a criminal or agitator or a would-be king. Then he let him go, as he had cured Pilate's wife when she was at the point of death.

Returning to his usual haunts he resumed his normal work. When the crowds grew bigger than ever, he earned by his actions an incomparable reputation. The exponents of the Law were mad with jealousy, and gave Pilate 30 talents to have him executed. Accepting the bribe, he gave them permission to carry out their wishes themselves. So they seized him and crucified him in defiance of all Jewish tradition.[2]

A first problem is to determine its genuineness.[3] Even if certainty is not possible, we should proceed in the first place as if the passage goes back to Josephus: if we cannot determine its origin, we should act on the basis that it is genuine Josephus to see what it may reveal. Then there is the argument of G. A. Williamson: "These records, like the famous allusions in *Antiquities*, are condemned as spurious by critics who, victims of their own wishful thinking and bent on destruction, are prepared without a trace of MS authority to bracket or reverse the meaning of any passage that conflicts with their pet theories. Such a proceeding is in the last degree unscientific. It is to be observed also that the forging of these passages for propaganda purposes could not have rendered the least service to a Christian apologist; they could never influence anyone not already convinced by the Gospels; they are in many important points irreconcilable with Christian tradition; and they clearly reveal their author not as a believer but as a doubting, if curious, onlooker."[4] Williamson also explains why the passages in question, including the one set out above, were omitted from the Greek text: "If then these passages are genuine, how did they come to be omitted from our Greek text? The answer is surely simple. If that text represents the final form of the book, an edition published when Domitian, the hater and persecutor of Christianity, was at the height of his power, would it not have been the last degree of folly—most improbable in one as careful of his own skin as Josephus—to include references to Christ as a benefactor and miracle-worker, something more than a man, unjustly condemned by Roman authority and perhaps raised from the dead, whose followers too had worked wonders and 'signs' beyond the power of medicine?"[5] Moreover, there is the obvious connection with another dubious passage of Josephus, this time from the Greek *Jewish Antiquities*:

18.63. About this time there lived Jesus, a wise man, if indeed one ought to call him a man, for he was a doer of marvelous feats, a teacher of such people as receive the truth with pleasure. He drew over to him many Jews and many Greeks. He was the Messiah. 64. When Pilate, upon hearing him accused by men of the highest standing among us, had condemned him to be crucified, those that loved him at the first did not give up this affection for him. For on the third day he appeared to them alive again, for the divine prophets had prophesied these and ten thousand other wonderful things about him. And the tribe of the Christians, so-called after him, has still not disappeared to this day.

Some scholars reject this passage altogether; the majority consider it in part interpolated and reconstruct it thus:

About this time there lived Jesus, a wise man for he was a doer of marvelous feats, a teacher of such men as receive the truth with pleasure. He drew over to him many Jews and many Greeks. When Pilate, upon hearing him accused by men of the highest standing among us, had condemned him to be crucified, those that loved him at the first did not give up their affection for him. And the tribe of the Christians, so-called after him, has still not disappeared to this day.[6]

The arguments for rejection or revision are that Josephus was a Pharisee and would not have called Jesus "χριστός," the Messiah. Moreover, the Christian writer, Origen, who lived from around 185 to 255, expressly states twice that Josephus did not believe in Jesus as the Christ.[7] Yet the passage is in all the manuscripts and was known to Eusebius around 324.[8] Further, the style seems to be very much that of Josephus, and there is a subsequent passage, *Jewish Antiquities* 20.200, that seems to imply that Jesus had already been introduced to the reader, which would not be the case if our passage had not existed: "And so he [Ananas] convened the judges of the Sanhedrin and brought before them a man named James, the brother of Jesus who was called the Christ, and some others."

The passages from the Slavonic Josephus and that dealing with Jesus in the *Jewish Antiquities* have a very different stance. Whatever approach one takes to the passage from the *Jewish Antiquities*, the argument for authenticity of the Slavonic *Jewish War* remains: it is inconceivable that a passage inserted at some stage into Josephus's *Jewish War*, whether in Slavonic or in Greek that was subsequently translated into Slavonic, should have some correspondence with a passage in the *Jewish Antiquities*, which itself was tampered with. That would involve an impossible editorial link between the two passages from two different works.[9]

Finally, there is a passage in the Slavonic Josephus that cannot have been written by a Christian of any persuasion or by any Jew who was not both doubting and inquisitive about Jesus: "However, in many ways he broke the law—for instance, he did not observe the Sabbath in the traditional manner. At the same time his conduct was beyond reproach. He did not need to use his hands: a word sufficed to fulfill his every purpose." No Christian would have been interested in whether Jesus used his hands (i.e., worked) to perform miracles on the Sabbath. And, most likely, once the Christians were separate from Jews, few Christians would know the wide scope of the Pharisees' interpretation of forbidden work. At the same time there is confusion in the text: "in many ways he broke the law"—"his conduct was beyond reproach." There is a keen expression of interest in Jesus here, and some bewilderment and even sympathy. These are not the words of a believing Jew once Christianity had come to be regarded as a threat. They seem the words of an earlier someone who has no axe to grind but is writing a historical account of the time: Josephus.

What then does the passage tell us? It gives, I suggest, a tradition about Jesus that was current in Pharisaic circles—Josephus, it will be recalled, was a Pharisee—and it has some correspondence with the Pharisaic narrative source in John that I have designated S. But Josephus's tradition is rather more favorable to Jesus and less so to the Jewish leaders. Jesus is a miracle worker, but still nothing more, and certainly not the Messiah.

The passage reveals a lot. Jesus was supremely apolitical. The people wanted him to destroy the Roman army and make himself king. But he took no notice. People regarded him as more than human, but there was no agreement as to who or what he was. His behavior on the Sabbath was noticeably untraditional and clearly aroused comment. Josephus contradicts himself here: Jesus broke the law in many ways, yet his conduct was beyond reproach. Josephus seems to be expressing the idea that has psychological strength, that to perform miracles on the Sabbath is to work. Yet he recognizes that Jesus did not work: he performed the miracles by the use of speech alone. As in John, the Jewish leaders are motivated in the first instance by anxiety that the Romans will intervene and crush the nation, but subsequently as in the Synoptic Gospels they have baser motives. Again, Pilate is represented as very loath to put Jesus to death. And Jesus is crucified.

But in the tradition recorded by Josephus there are implausible elements. Thus, had many followers of Jesus been butchered by the Romans, some trace would have survived in the Gospels.

The Gospels' version that the followers melted away is much more likely: apart from anything else, it does not show the early followers of Jesus in a good light; hence it is unlikely to be a Christian invention. Moreover, if Jesus' followers had resisted and been butchered, Pilate would scarcely have released him as beneficial. Again, that the Jews and not the Romans crucified Jesus is not credible. As Josephus well knew, crucifixion was contrary to Jewish custom. There is also the testimony of the Gospels and of Tacitus that it was Pilate who had Jesus executed. Still, there is an ambiguity in the Synoptic Gospels, most noticeably in Matthew, that indicates that such a tradition could arise:

> Matthew 27.24. So when Pilate saw that he could do nothing, but rather that a riot was beginning, he took some water and washed his hands before the crowd, saying, "I am innocent of this man's blood; see to it yourselves." 25. Then the people as a whole answered, "His blood be on us and on our children!" 26. So he released Barabbas for them; and after flogging Jesus, he handed him over to be crucified.

Pilate said to the Jews, "See to it yourselves," and he handed Jesus over.[10] A version such as this could easily give rise to the notion that it was the Jews who crucified Jesus. There is a further Jewish element here: hand washing as a gesture of innocence of spilling innocent blood is a Jewish, not a Roman, habit.[11] Is it merely a coincidence that in Josephus Pilate's wife intervened in an attempt to save Jesus, as she did also in Matthew? I am inclined to suspect rather some shared tradition. There is yet another connection with Matthew. As Robert Grant has insisted,[12] for the redactor of Matthew Jesus is the new Moses: "Just as Pharaoh tried to kill all the sons born to the Hebrews (Exod. 1.22), so Herod slew the little boys of Bethlehem (Matt.

2.16); but both Moses and Jesus escaped (compare Matt. 2.14 with Exod. 2.15). After the king's death both Moses and Jesus returned to the lands where they were to do God's work (Exod. 2.23; 4.19; Matt. 2.19–20). From a mountain top both Moses and Jesus delivered the law which God had given them (Exod. 19–20; Matt. 5.1). In the sermon on the mount Jesus states that he has come to 'fulfill' the law of Moses, from which no smallest fragment shall pass away until the end of the age (5.17–18)." And in the Slavonic Josephus some people thought Jesus was the first lawgiver—that is, Moses—risen from the dead.

In Josephus, Pilate's final participation is awkward and seems unnecessary. Apparently the tradition of Roman involvement was too strong to keep him out.

The Slavonic Josephus thus turns out to be extremely important for our understanding of the early traditions about the life of Jesus. These traditions were sometimes conflicting, but also connected and intertwined. As we saw earlier in this book, when the tradition behind Mark was the main one, there could still be disagreements about certain episodes. And Matthew and Luke show that, with regard to these disagreements, there could be several conflicting voices.

The Jewish non-Christian pro-Roman hellenized Josephus knew a tradition about Jesus. This tradition shares with S in John the view that Jesus was a miracle worker but not the Messiah, and that the Jewish leaders had him arrested because they feared that the Romans would intervene and destroy them. The tradition shares with Matthew a connection between Jesus and Moses, Jesus teaching on the Mount of Olives (Matthew 24.3),[13] a role for Pilate's wife in an attempt to spare Jesus, absolute responsibility of the Jewish leaders for the Crucifixion, and a backseat for Pilate. But above all, the Slavonic Josephus shares with all the Gospels the tradition that Jesus was supremely uninterested in secular politics. Josephus was so hostile to the Zealots that, if Jesus had been believed to have any connection with them, Josephus would have discussed it and given a very different picture of him.

That the tradition in Josephus has points of contact with the tradition in both S and Matthew may indicate that when the Synoptics disagree among themselves this may not be because one tradition was prevalent in one place and another in another, but that different traditions circulated together, and the evangelists made choices. We should accept that there were many related yet often contradictory traditions about Jesus.

Finally for Josephus it should be noted that Jesus appears only as a miracle worker and not also as a teacher (though he had unorthodox views about the Sabbath).

11

✠

JOHN:
THE
CORRECTIVE
TO
MARK

✠ ✠ ✠

AS IS ADMITTED ON ALL HANDS, JOHN IS A VERY DIF-
ferent Gospel from the Synoptics. I believe that the main narrative source in John was a Pharisaic tradition that was too well
known in the community to be ignored. Instead, I believe, the
compiler took the Pharisaic source, changed it slightly, added a
particular theological message, and tried to make it harmless for
Christian belief. Still, as is the case with composite works, the
separate strands can to some extent be disentangled when one
looks for inconsistencies or details that appear contrary to the
main message. The Pharisaic source, which I designate S, can
most easily be spotted in the realistic details for which John is as
remarkable as for his ecstatic theology. S represents Jesus as a
miracle worker, but certainly not the Messiah, and as a human

being who not only was hostile to Jewish religious customs but was also deeply flawed as a man.

The character of much of the narrative in John turns out to be useful in evaluating Mark. In some respects, as I noted earlier, these Gospels have characteristics in common that are not shared with Matthew and Luke. In Mark and John, Jesus is much more confrontational. In Mark 2, at the outset of his ministry, Jesus is aggressive to the Pharisees; in John 2, Jesus' behavior at the cleansing of the Temple, at the beginning of his ministry, is outrageous toward all observing Jews, though afterwards his main targets are the Pharisees. In both Mark and John the Pharisees react with great restraint. In both, the Sanhedrin does not convict Jesus. Since John is so unlike the Synoptics, I believe I see in these characteristics elements of a tradition that goes a long way back. To that extent, John confirms the historicity of Mark: Jesus provoking conflict with the Pharisees, their moderation, and the failure of the Sanhedrin to convict. The only explanation that seems plausible is that there is an early stratum of tradition which existed when Mark was written and which survived later in the community where John was composed, but which had been lost in the communities where Matthew and Luke were set down, where Jewish historical memory was less pronounced.

Conversely, this takes us back to an argument set out earlier in this book: that not infrequently Matthew and Luke diverge at the same places from Mark on whom they rely for the basic text. Jesus is less aggressive, the Pharisees are more confrontational, and the Sanhedrin is more corrupt. What emerges is a dynamic shift among Christians in their own tradition. It must not be forgotten that when Matthew and Luke diverge from Mark in the same places they do not always do so in the same way. But some traits in Mark had become no longer wholly acceptable.

The change in tradition appears nowhere more clearly than in the behavior of Pontius Pilate. In all four Gospels he is reluctant to execute Jesus, but especially so in Matthew and Luke. In Matthew he washes his hands of it before the crowd and says, "I am innocent of this man's blood; see to it yourselves" (27.24). In Luke, Pilate even tries to pass the buck by sending Jesus to Herod Antipas (23.6ff.). But Pilate has no reason to involve himself, because in these two Gospels the Sanhedrin has condemned Jesus—though in Luke after only one morning session—and the Jewish leaders could put him to death themselves. Matthew and Luke want to diminish Roman involvement in Jesus' death, but they cannot depart from the tradition. It was undeniable, after all, that it was the Romans who crucified him. Mark's account is rather more plausible. The Jewish leaders who wanted Jesus dead had no choice in Mark but to accuse him before Pilate of a secular crime because they themselves, for technical rules of evidence, had been unable to convict. Pilate was reluctant, but only until he established that the crowd wanted Jesus executed, not saved. Thereafter, he exhibited no hesitation. John takes a very different tack because of the use made of S.[1] It exculpates the Jewish leaders to a considerable extent. After Jesus raises Lazarus from the dead (John 11.12–44), the Sanhedrin holds a meeting that is not a trial. The leaders have a genuine problem. If Jesus can raise one man from the dead, might he not raise a whole army? The chief priests say: "What are we to do? This man is performing many signs. If we let him go on like this, everyone will believe in him, and the Romans will come and destroy both our holy place and our nation" (John 11.47f.). The fear was reasonable. If the people believed Jesus was the Messiah, they would believe he would lead them against the Romans—that was in the nature of the Messiah. But if Jesus was not in fact the Messiah, the Romans would with their immense strength crush the revolt and destroy the Temple and the

Jewish nation. Caiaphas, the high priest, interjects: "You do not understand that it is better for you to have one man die for the people than to have the whole nation destroyed" (John 11.50). This interjection should not be treated as cynical even though it is self-serving. Caiaphas's point is part of a rabbinic debate that has been expounded by David Daube.[2] What are Jews to do when ruffians or enemy forces demand the surrender of one of them under the threat of otherwise killing them all? The initial stance of the Pharisees, evidenced for A.D. 66,[3] was that no one was to be surrendered. That position was untenable and had to be modified. If the enemy demanded a named individual, he could be surrendered, but Jews must not comply with an order for themselves to choose and then surrender an unnamed person. In the present case the Jews are under an occupying power who, according to John, have taken away the Sanhedrin's power to impose the death penalty. But the Jews have in their midst a troublemaker who, if he proceeds untouched, will cause their total destruction. The Romans have not asked for his surrender. What should the Jewish leaders do? Presumably the Pharisees opposed surrender to the Romans whereas Caiaphas argued for it. For me this version derives from S; its purpose is to justify the behavior of the Jewish leaders. In John there is no Jewish trial. Still, John provides the most plausible explanation for Pilate becoming involved: a covert threat that he would suffer the disfavor of the emperor if he did not execute Jesus for sedition.

> John 19.12. From then on Pilate tried to release him, but the Jews cried out, "If you release this man, you are no friend of the emperor. Everyone who claims to be a king sets himself against the emperor."

John provides an important corrective to Mark in the episode of the cleansing of the Temple even though John's timing is impossible.[4] He correctly identifies the victims—the money changers and sellers of animals and birds for sacrifice (John 2.13ff.). He thus points to the real victims: Sadducees, Pharisees, and all observing Jews. Violence is an integral part of the scene. Even if we believe, as I do not, that John exaggerates the violence, it still seems obvious that Mark plays down the extent of the violence and the full insult to all Jews. He thus casts a veil over Jesus' motivation—to bring about his own death at the hands of the Jewish religious authorities.

Mark and John each offer insights into the composition of the other. Mark is the earliest Gospel, so we must say something about its raison d'être, especially because it is a very mysterious work. The stress is on the Passion, but before that, Jesus' teaching and his miracles are emphasized. Strangely, however, the message in Jesus' teaching is underemphasized, is usually unclear, and, at that, is deliberately confusing, though the miracles are an integral part of the teaching. At times the performance of miracles seems to take over from any particular message. How can that be, especially since Mark came to be a model?

The answer is belief in the Resurrection. This justifies everything for Mark. The precise meaning of the message is insignificant, except that salvation comes through faith in Jesus. And the Resurrection justifies the faith.

It is no paradox that less emphasis is placed on the Resurrection in Mark than in the other Gospels. (I accept completely the opinion that Mark originally ended at 16.8).[5] Emphasis for Mark is not needed because one of those who saw the risen Jesus was Peter, and the author of Mark was the companion, Mark, a follower and interpreter of Peter. Mark had personal information from one whom he trusted, someone who had seen the Resurrection. This is the standard opinion of both ancient authorities[6] and modern scholarship.[7]

It is a work like Mark that explains the existence of John—

or more precisely, the narrative tradition in John that derives from S. For those Jews who did not accept the Resurrection, a work such as Mark had to be countered. Hence from the earliest time after Jesus' death there existed and developed a tradition that culminated in works like S. The same episodes that are found in early Christian works would appear in Jewish narratives but with differing emphases and conclusions. In those narratives Jesus, who had appeared to some to be the Messiah, had shown the world by his death that he was not. He was a miracle worker: so much could easily be conceded. But he was also a charismatic charlatan who had no moral or religious message. It will be recalled how difficult it is to find a moral or religious message in Mark: what is required is faith, faith which is justified by the Resurrection. In these Jewish narratives Jesus was hostile from the outset to Jewish religious practices and to the Pharisees, who were their main proponents. He was a flawed human being who was given to outbursts of rage, even against his mother, and he obstructed the religious observance of others. In the end, his behavior made him a danger to the very existence of the Temple and of the Jewish people.

12

✠

THE
MESSIAH,
THE SON
OF
DAVID

✠ ✠ ✠

I HAVE INSISTED MORE THAN ONCE IN THIS VOLUME
on the tight construction of the Gospel of Mark. The four questions put to Jesus in Mark 12.13–37 are another prime example.
Their nature was elucidated by David Daube.[1]

> [T]he rabbis knew a classification of questions into four
> types; it is evidenced in an anecdote involving a leading
> scholar of the half-century following the destruction of
> the Temple,[2] and it is used in an early section of the Hag-
> gadha.[3] (1) "Questions of wisdom," about points of law;
> (2) "questions of vulgarity," mocking questions, principally
> about bodily resurrection, by which the questioner cuts
> himself off from the community—will the dead need sprin-
> kling when they rise, having been in contact with corpses?

(3) "questions of the proper way of the land," about the basis of simple piety; and (4) "questions of interpretation," about apparent contradictions in Scripture—one passage saying that God has chosen Zion, another that he has rejected it. Manifestly the four questions in Mark represent the four types: (1) law, tribute to Caesar, (2) mockery, the widow of seven, (3) simple piety, the first commandment, (4) contradictions, the Messiah David's son and Lord.

I remarked in a previous chapter that the Sadducees who put question two could scarcely have been deeply interested in Jesus' answer.[4] Now we see that it was contrived or retained by the author of Mark to fit the fourfold scheme. Our concern here, though, is with the fourth question:

Mark 12.35. While Jesus was teaching in the temple, he said, "How can the scribes say that the Messiah is the son of David? 36. David himself, by the Holy Spirit, declared,

'The Lord said to my Lord,
"Sit at my right hand,
until I put your enemies under your feet." '

37. David himself calls him Lord; so how can he be his son?" And the large crowd was listening to him with delight.

The interpretation has caused problems. Vincent Taylor writes, "The narrative indicates, although obscurely, the mind of Jesus on the question of Messiahship."[5] But he does not say how it does so. C. E. B. Cranfield expounds on the words, "How can the scribes say that the Messiah is the Son of David?"

As the section stands, it appears as if Jesus introduced the subject on his own initiative. But it seems unlikely that he would have done so; for he would hardly have introduced it as a merely academic question, and that he introduced it with a clear reference to himself is even more unlikely. Moreover, it is most improbable that he would have attacked a doctrine so firmly based on scripture as that of the Davidic descent of the Messiah (e.g., Isa. ix. 2–7, xi. 1–9; Jer. xxiii. 5f., xxxiii. 14–18, Ezek. xxxiv. 23f., xxxvii. 24); had he done so, the fact would surely have been brought up against him (but of this there is no trace) and this doctrine would hardly have been so established an element of the Church's faith as it was (e.g., Rom. i. 3., 2 Tim. ii. 8). On the other hand, the unanimity of early Christian tradition about Jesus' Davidic descent makes it most unlikely that this saying is the creation of the early Church.

The best explanation seems to be that of R. P. Gagg, that the section is the remains of an original conflict-story, the opening question of which has been lost in the course of tradition. A question whether he taught that the Messiah would be David's son could have been part of his opponents' attack (cf. xii. 13ff., xii. 18ff.). It could have been asked in the hope that it might lead Jesus into saying something which could be used to incriminate him with the Romans or else possibly something which could be used to discredit him in the eyes of the people. Jesus then replies, as in other conflict-stories, not with a direct answer, but with a counter-question. His purpose is not to impart teaching but to escape a trap by breaking off the conversation.[6]

The problems that interpreters face are confirmed by C. S. Mann:

We are accustomed to regarding this questioning by Jesus along with the quotation from Ps 110 in v. 36 as though it was used by Jesus as proof of his Davidic descent. But it is just as easily interpreted as casting doubt on the whole idea. That the expected messiah-deliverer would be of Davidic lineage was a commonplace in some sectors of Judaism and could claim Old Testament support, and among the Essenes a priestly messiah and a Davidic (kingly) messiah were expected. But in either case, publicly to court a messianic title was an invitation to Roman intervention. By asking the question, Jesus was inviting his critics to question one possible assumption—that he was a perfervid nationalist seeking to enlist popular support. By the time Mark's gospel was finally committed to writing the kind of question posed by Jesus had been overtaken not only by the events of the final week of the ministry but also by the first stirrings of the Jewish revolt against Rome. By then, Jewish Christians had either fled or were under pressure to declare themselves for or against the nationalist cause.[7]

None of the explanations that have been quoted seem at all plausible.[8] Fortunately for our purposes it does not matter whether Jesus himself posed the question or whether it was a trap question put to him—though the former is the real probability[9]—because one problem for an understanding, which is also the key to understanding, has been overlooked. Verse 37 ends: "And the large crowd was listening to him with delight." Why on earth should Jesus' complicated answer cause the crowd to rejoice? The reason is that Jesus was in effect revealing himself to the crowd as the Messiah.

The question is the fourth question, concerning contradictions: scriptural texts indicate the Messiah will be a descendant of David. Jesus produces an argument from another text, Psalm

110.1, that the Messiah will not be a descendant of David. Many Jews would have seen that Jesus had most of the fundamental qualities to be recognized as king of the Jews from God or the Messiah. If he were, he would destroy the Romans, and this, we can assume, the people would want. But what is lacking among traditional messianic features is Jesus' descent from David. Mark says nothing about Jesus' genealogy. Now Jesus is saying that the Messiah will not descend from David. Since the crowd wants to accept him as the Messiah, they believe him. And they rejoice.

The problems in understanding have largely arisen because the episode occurs also in Matthew 22.41–46 and Luke 20.41–44. And Jesus' descent from David is spelled out in Matthew 1.1ff. and Luke 3.23ff. But the Synoptic Gospels should not be linked together indiscriminately. Nothing in Mark suggests that Jesus descended from David. The genealogy in Matthew and Luke is in any event inappropriate because the descent from David is traced through Joseph, and in neither of these Gospels is Joseph the father of Jesus.[10] Again, neither Matthew nor Luke has anything that corresponds to Mark's "And the large crowd was listening to him with delight." I would once more see this as a weakening of Mark's standpoint, a failure to understand.

In Mark 12.35ff., Jesus has come very close to declaring to the people that he is the Messiah. At the least he has dropped a very large hint.[11] The accuracy of this interpretation of Mark is confirmed by Acts 2.29–36. The apostle Peter is speaking:

29. "Fellow Israelites, I may say to you confidently of our ancestor David that he both died and was buried, and his tomb is with us to this day. 30. Since he was a prophet, he knew that God had sworn with an oath to him that he

would put one of his descendants on his throne. 31. Foreseeing this, David spoke of the resurrection of the Messiah, saying,

'He was not abandoned to Hades,
nor did his flesh experience corruption.'

32. This Jesus God raised up, and of that all of us are witnesses. 33. Being therefore exalted at the right hand of God, and having received from the Father the promise of the Holy Spirit, he has poured out this that you both see and hear. 34. For David did not ascend into the heavens, but he himself says,

'The Lord said to my Lord,
"Sit at my right hand,
35. until I make your enemies your footstool." '

36. Therefore let the entire house of Israel know with certainty that God has made him both Lord and Messiah, this Jesus whom you crucified."

Thus, the same obscure text is used, by Peter this time, as proof that Jesus was the Messiah. The importance of this passage is increased if the author of Acts is, as is generally believed, the author of Luke.[12] Luke, I have claimed, fails to see the point of Jesus' use of the text. Moreover, Luke traces Jesus' descent from David, which would turn reliance on the text for Jesus being the Messiah into nonsense. Now we have in Acts the verses just quoted where the text is used again to show that Jesus is the Messiah. But the argument from the text is incomprehensible, as will be seen by a glance at standard commentaries.[13] As in Luke, so in Acts, the evangelist does not understand the point of the text, but he uses it because it is in the tradition. The author of Acts shows at 2.30 that he believes the Messiah will be a descendant of David. All that emerges from the quotation from Psalm 110.1 in Acts is that the text somehow proves that Jesus is the Messiah.[14] The interpretation I have given of Mark explains why the text is used for that purpose.

13

✠

WHAT
REALLY
HAPPENED

✠ ✠ ✠

WHAT REALLY HAPPENED? IN THIS FIELD THERE ARE various possible degrees of knowledge.[1] At the high end I would put historical certainty, and I would place within it that there was such a person as Jesus, who was crucified by the Romans on orders of Pontius Pilate, and that somehow some highly placed Jews were involved in his death. At the low end I would place traditions whose ultimate source is unverifiable: here I would include Caiaphas's question whether Jesus was the Messiah and Pilate's question whether Jesus was the king of the Jews. Who was present who reported the questions to people who were the ultimate builders of the tradition? Are we to give credit to the interpreters whom we can assume to have been present? Still, when that has been said, the questions are likely enough. Caiaphas would certainly want to know whether Jesus thought he was the Messiah, and certainly Pilate would want to know if Jesus claimed to be king of the Jews. For knowledge of this kind we must proceed from the evidence of the surviving sources always within the context of knowledge at the high end of the scale. The methodology here is no different from the weighing of evidence for other aspects of the history of the Roman empire. From the arguments in previous chapters it will be obvious that I will take the Gospel of Mark as the basis of my reconstruction of what happened according to the best later tradition.

Jesus was quite uninterested in secular politics. Above all, he paid no attention to the troublesome issue of Roman occupation of Judaea and the client status of Herod Antipas, tetrarch of Galilee. Though Galileans were prominent among the Zealots, the fact that Galilee was not under direct Roman rule could make it possible for a Galilean, like Jesus, to be more detached. Jesus was no Zealot or any equivalent for his time, and, at the least, he was not troubled in his conscience by the Roman occupation of Judaea. He was also not much moved by the main argument of the Zealots against the Romans, that by paying taxes to the Romans the Jews accepted the Romans as their rulers and thus broke their covenant with God that he would be the only lord of Israel. When Jesus was asked if it were lawful to pay taxes to the Romans, his very astute answer was, at least prima facie, that it was. Those skilled in dialectic, as the Pharisees were who had put the question, would notice that his wording could mean the opposite: what was God's was to be given to God, but everything was God's. Still, he had said nothing that was hostile to the Romans.

Jesus taught "with authority" (Mark 1.22ff.), thus in a way that somehow seemed unlike that of the rabbis.[2] What his message was is usually obscure, to say the least, but the performance of miracles was an integral part of the message, as is made plain from his earliest ministry (Mark 1.24ff.). Still, even from the beginning he did not want simply to be regarded as a miracle worker and, at times, he was at pains to hide the miracle. Or, at least, he said the miracle was to be concealed, thus heightening the drama while ensuring that knowledge of it would be spread.

Jesus was the charismatic religious authority, and as such was always likely to be in conflict with the main institutional religious authority, the Pharisees. But it was Jesus who engineered the confrontation. He was preaching his message—again it is noticeable that the spiritual nature of the message is not recorded—when he told a paralytic that his sins were forgiven (Mark 2.5). The statement is striking: Jesus had provided no evidence for it, and it was not linked with any preceding miracle; and no ordinary human could either forgive sin directly or understand the mind of God. Scribes who were present not unnaturally regarded the words as blasphemous, but they did not say so. Jesus confronted them, brought up the issue, and asked if it were easier to say, "Your sins are forgiven" or "Take your bed, and walk" (Mark 2.9).[3]

Then he cured the man (with the less offensive formulation) in order, he said, that they might know that the Son of man (i.e., himself) had power on earth to forgive sin (Mark 2.10f.). Whatever justification Jesus felt he had, or indeed had, this stance was abrasive in the extreme and was meant to be. All that Jesus had shown was that he could perform miracles. But miracle workers were very common and were usually believed to be little more than that, miracle workers. Thereafter, the Pharisees followed him to see what he would do, but they made no attempt to entrap him. Rather, they were interested in knowing what his authority was and whether he was like them or was a charlatan.

They saw him reclining at dinner in the house of Levi with sinners and asked why he did so (Mark 2.15ff.). Their attitude was not unreasonable: to recline at dinner rather than sit showed that the occasion was festive, and a holy person should not eat with those uncaring of ritual or enter the house of one who might not have paid the tithe.

Again, they noticed his disciples did not fast, and they asked why (Mark 2.18ff.). Voluntary fasting had become an outward sign of piety. So why did Jesus' disciples not fast? The Pharisees asked why his disciples plucked grain on the Sabbath, a breach of the prohibition on working (2.23ff.). Again, this was a most reasonable question from Pharisees, who upheld the oral law and who wanted to understand Jesus. Jesus' reply was legalistic and unconvincing. He tried to justify a breach of halakah by an appeal to haggadah. But for the Pharisees, a breach of halakah could be justified only by an appeal to a conflicting rule of halakah, not by haggadah. If we accept the distinction between halakah and haggadah, then logic is entirely on the side of the Pharisees. Nonetheless, the response of the Pharisees was muted. We are not even told what it was. But they still watched him (Mark 3.1ff.). They wanted to see if he would cure a withered hand on the Sabbath so that they could accuse him. The centrality of the Sabbath is of paramount importance to the Pharisees: without the Sabbath, there is no Judaism. It is possible to cure without breaching the prohibition on working, but the probability is against it. Certainly, the psychological presumption must be that a cure would breach the Sabbath. But Jesus did not at first cure. Instead, he again attacked verbally, asking if it were lawful to do good or harm on the Sabbath, to save life or to kill. The question is palpably unfair. It would be just as unlawful—to say the least—to do evil and to kill by working on the Sabbath. Besides, in certain circumstances, work on the Sabbath was lawful. This was especially true when a life was endangered; contrary to the implication of Jesus' question, it was permissible to work on the Sabbath to save a life.[4]

But Jesus' hostility to the Pharisees was verbalized and manifest. He then cured the hand, and the Pharisees conspired with the Herodians to kill him. They overreacted, but Jesus was a direct challenge and threat to their institutional religious authority. And that was his intention. The Pharisees recognized that he was implacably hostile.

Despite further miracles (Mark 3.10ff.), Jesus still had not convinced the crowd—not to say the Pharisees—of his special authority. On the contrary, the people were saying, "He has gone out of his mind" (Mark 3.21). Even his family thought they might have to put restraints upon him. The scribes suggested that he cast out demons by the ruler of the demons (Mark 3.22). Jesus' response was to put a rhetorical question, followed by not easily comprehensible parables. Jesus was not trying to make friends by being placatory or even persuasive. Nor to this point has he divulged a clear religious message. He becomes more outrageous. People, he says, will be forgiven their sins and their blasphemies, but those who blaspheme against him—he says "the Holy Spirit," but the context shows he means himself— can never be forgiven (Mark 3.28f.). Quite unsurprisingly, the crowd and his family still think he is insane (Mark 3.31ff.).

He teaches in parables that are, and astoundingly are meant to be, incomprehensible (Mark 4.1ff.). In fact, he claims that he is deliberately obscure so that people will not understand, will not turn again, and so will not be forgiven (Mark 4.11f.). He explains only to his disciples (Mark 4.10f, 33f.), but at times even they did not understand Jesus' message. They also could not understand that the wind and the sea obeyed him (Mark 4.41).

Jesus continued to perform miracles. He drove a legion of demons out of a man and into a herd of pigs (Mark 5.1ff.), with the effect that the people of the neighborhood begged him to leave (Mark 5.17). As anything more than a miracle worker, Jesus was a distinct failure. He had conveyed nothing of himself as a spiritual leader. He appeared so threatening, in fact, that ordinary people were just desperate for him to leave, even in response to a miracle.

At this stage, indeed, Jesus seemed to be concentrating on miracles, and he had given up on any spiritual message, whether he had one, could not communicate it, or did not want to communicate it. Instead he brought to life the daughter of Jairus (Mark 5.21ff., 35ff.) and healed a woman who had been hemorrhaging for twelve years (Mark 5.25ff.).

When Jesus teaches in his hometown, Nazareth—again we are told nothing of his message—the members of the congregation are amazed because they know his family, and he offends them (Mark 6.1ff.). He sends out his disciples with authority to cast out unclean spirits—more miracles—and to teach repentance (Mark 6.7ff.). Again, the nature of the teaching is not stated. Jesus performs the miracle of the loaves and fishes (Mark 6.34ff.), and he walks on water (Mark 6.47ff.). The disciples are astounded: they do not understand about the loaves, and their hearts are hardened (Mark 6.51f.). Jesus heals many (Mark 6.53ff.).

The Pharisees follow him (Mark 7.1ff.) and ask why his disciples do not follow tradition but eat with unwashed hands. In fury, Jesus calls them hypocrites who teach human precepts but abandon God's commands (Mark 7.5ff.).

Jesus tells the crowd that nothing outside a person makes him unclean by going in (Mark 7.14ff.). Privately he tells his disciples that by this incomprehensible teaching he means that no food is unclean (Mark 7.17ff.). The moral importance of this teaching about food is not stated, nor is it self-evident. Still, it is obviously a contradiction of the Mosaic law. (His private teaching to the disciples does have an obvious moral base, but the morality could be taught without any allusion to no food being unclean.) He cures the daughter of a Gentile woman (Mark 7.25ff.) but only after roughly advising her that his ministry is to the Jews: he likens Jews to children, all others to dogs. He cures a deaf man with a speech impediment (Mark 7.32ff.). His attention is still focused only on performing miracles. He performs another miracle with loaves and fishes (Mark 8.1ff.). The Pharisees ask for a sign from heaven (Mark 8.11ff.). Indeed, they have every justification for wondering where his miracles come from, unaccompanied as they now are by any explicit message. Jesus refuses (Mark 8.11ff.). He tells the disciples to beware of the yeast of the Pharisees and of Herod (Mark 8.14ff.). So confusing is he that the disciples think he is referring to the miracle of the loaves. Jesus says, "Do you not yet understand?" (Mark 8.21). We are not told their response, but we know it. They are totally confused.

Jesus cures a blind man, but wants it kept secret (Mark 8.22ff.). He teaches his disciples that the Son of man (himself) must undergo suffering, be rejected by the chief priests, the scribes, and the elders, be put to death, and after three days rise again (Mark 8.31ff.).[5] Peter, who does not understand, rebukes him and is rebuked in his turn: "Get behind me, Satan! For you are setting your mind not on divine things but on human things" (Mark 8.32f.). But Jesus does not explain to Peter. Moreover, the second sentence in the quotation shows that "Get you behind me, Satan" is not a generalized outcry against temptation or evil. Jesus is actually calling Peter "Satan." Jesus shows little control in his vituperation, even toward a favored disciple.

Then:

Mark 8.34. He called the crowd with his disciples, and said to them, "If any want to become my followers, let them deny themselves and take up their cross and follow me. 35. For those who want to save their life will lose it, and those who lose their life for my sake, and for the sake of the gospel, will save it. 36. For what will it profit them to gain the whole world and forfeit their life? 37. Indeed, what can they give in return for their life? 38. Those who are ashamed of me and of my words in this adulterous and sinful generation, of them the Son of man will also be ashamed when he comes in the glory of his Father with the holy angels."

This wonderful charismatic speech is indecipherable (except perhaps with hindsight). No meaning can be extracted from it, except that one should follow Jesus. But in what? And how? The charismatic, incomprehensible, ecstatic address is a genuine characteristic of Jesus. What is virtually a parody of it— actually I would go further—and is confirmation that this is an important side of Jesus is in John 3.1ff. There the good Pharisee, Nicodemus the seeker after truth, visits Jesus at night and says he knows Jesus is from God. Before he has a chance to explain what he wants to know, Jesus interrupts rudely and not apropos: "Very truly, I tell you, no one can see the kingdom of God without being born from above" (John 3.3). Understandably, Nicodemus misunderstands and thinks Jesus is saying one must be born again. (In Greek, ἄνωθεν can mean both "from above" and "again.") Jesus gives no credit to Nicodemus' good intentions, and we have a speech, ecstatic but incomprehensible, which is nasty to Nicodemus (John 3.10) and not geared to his well-being.[6]

Someone who had a son possessed by a demon which prevented him from speaking brings him to Jesus, whom he addresses as "Teacher" (Mark 9.14ff.). Again, Jesus vents his fury: "You faithless generation, how much longer must I be among you? How much longer must I put up with you? Bring him to me" (Mark 9.19). Jesus cures the boy but with a very ill grace. But why should a parent, no matter how strong his faith, not want to have his son cured? And Jesus is now a noted miracle worker. Jesus' whole attitude seems staged, to heighten the drama of the cure.

Jesus continues to teach, still in an unclear manner (Mark 9.42ff.). He insists, however, that children should be welcome in his name (Mark 9.37), and no stumbling block shall be put in the way of children who believe in him (Mark 9.42). Children are being brought for him to touch and his disciples speak sternly to them (Mark 10.13).

> Mark 10.14. But when Jesus saw this, he was indignant and said to them, "Let the little children come to me; do not stop them; for it is to such as these that the kingdom of God belongs. 15. Truly I tell you, whoever does not receive the kingdom of God as a child will never enter it." 16. And he took them up in his arms, laid his hands on them, and blessed them.

At this stage of his ministry, Jesus appears to be taking a special interest in children to further their belief in him.

A rich man asks what is needed for eternal life (Mark 10.17ff.), and Jesus tells him to sell what he owns, give the money to the poor, and follow him. This is the first time in Mark that Jesus seems to express a charitable, social purpose. In a very puzzling way even for the disciples, Jesus claims it is difficult for a rich man to enter the kingdom of God (Mark 10.23ff.): "For mortals it is impossible, but not for God; for God all things are possible" (Mark 10.27).

Jesus and his disciples are on the road to Jerusalem (Mark 10.32ff.), and Jesus walks ahead of them—a sign of resolution. He takes them aside, and says:

10.33. "See, we are going up to Jerusalem, and the Son of Man will be handed over to the chief priests and the scribes, and they will condemn him to death; then they will hand him over to the Gentiles; 34. they will mock him, and spit upon him, and flog him, and kill him; and after three days he will rise again."

There is more to this than prophesy with hindsight. This is the first time[7] that Jesus goes to Jerusalem. He is going in the belief that he will be put to death—and even with the intention that he be put to death.

At this stage it is time to consider what characteristics Jesus shares with other charismatic religious authorities and even with fanatical secular leaders. There is first of all the claim that the only way to "salvation" is through faith in him. Complete faith in the leader personally is the essential requirement. Second, the leader separates his followers from their families: this is regarded as a standard feature of modern cults. Thus in Mark:

10.29. Jesus said: "Truly I tell you, there is no one who has left house or brothers or sisters or mother or father or children or fields, for my sake and for the sake of the good news, 30. who will not receive a hundredfold now in this age—houses, brothers and sisters, mothers and children, and fields with persecutions—and in the age to come eternal life."

Even more striking is Luke:

14.26. "Whoever comes to me and does not hate father and mother, wife and children, brothers and sisters, yes, and even life itself, cannot be my disciple."

The Gospel of Thomas (§§ 55 and 101) likewise claims that those who do not hate mother and father cannot become disciples of Jesus.[8] Third, there is the leader's performance of miracles, and for this performance the importance of faith on the part of the beneficiaries is stressed. Thus, in his hometown, Nazareth, Jesus could do no deed of power except cure a few people (Mark 6.1ff.). Jesus is amazed at the people's unbelief. Fourth, there is the message couched in high-flown rhetoric, made deliberately obscure, not fully comprehended even by the closest followers, and perhaps ultimately either incomprehensible or of little meaning. Fifth, in a very deep sense, women understand him: in Mark there is the woman who had been hemorrhaging for twelve years (5.25ff.) and the woman who anointed him (14.3ff.). Sixth, there is the emphasis on children and on their faith. Seventh, there is the deliberate challenge to, and provoking of, the established institutional authority. Eighth, there is the prediction that his followers will be persecuted and even killed because of their belief in him.[9] Ninth, there is the avowal of followers—in this case, Peter—that they will suffer death rather than deny the leader.[10] Tenth, the followers arm themselves and are prepared to use their weapons.[11] Last, there is the leader's prediction that enemies will seek to kill him but that death will not be the end. There is what seems to be a deliberate courting of this death—a courting that need not be present at the beginning of the mission.

Leaving Jericho (Mark 10.46ff.), Jesus cures blind Bartimaeus, saying, "Go: your faith has made you well" (Mark 10.52). On the way to Jerusalem Jesus has a tumultuous welcome from the crowd (Mark 11.8ff.), which treats him as someone with a special relationship with God. This is the first time Jesus has won widespread recognition not simply as a miracle worker but as someone whose power is from God. It is also the last during his lifetime.

Here we must put three questions to which the answers have

varying degrees of probability. First, and this is the least important question, did Jesus ever directly say he was the Messiah? I think the answer is probably no. Second, did Jesus believe he was the Messiah or have some very particular connection with God? The answer is almost certainly yes; otherwise, his behavior is inexplicable. Third, did people believe he was the Messiah? The answer must be that at this stage some did or at least had high hopes that he was. The fears that, miracle worker as he was, he had come from the devil had given way to rejoicing.[12] It should be remembered that in the Slavonic Josephus, many thought he would drive out the Romans and make himself king: that is, they thought he was the Messiah. Moreover, later, after the cleansing of the Temple, at the fourth question, Jesus came very close to declaring publicly that he was the Messiah. Again, the Eucharistic details in the Last Supper in the Synoptics show Jesus indirectly claiming to his disciples to be the Messiah. In all probability, Jesus' style, combined with the Jews' historical longing for political freedom, contributed to a belief that he was the Messiah. Acts 1.6 indicates that after the Crucifixion the apostles hoped and expected that the risen Jesus would restore the kingdom to Israel.

Mark 14.36 also indicates that Jesus considered himself to be the Messiah. After the Passover dinner Jesus went to Gethsemane with his disciples (Mark 14.32). He told the others to sit but took Peter, James, and John with him and told them to stay awake (Mark 14.33f.). He prayed in great distress (Mark 14.35). "Abba, Father, for you all things are possible; remove this cup from me; yet, not what I want, but what you want" (Mark 14.36). Afterward he found the three disciples sleeping. The rabbinic rule was that the Passover celebration was ended when some of the company fell sound asleep.[13] Jesus was now spiritually alone.

But to the prayer. The common opinion is that this is in two antithetical parts—wish, surrender—and is the quintessence of all prayer. But David Daube has correctly pointed out that the structure is not twofold but threefold: it starts out with the acknowledgment that with God all things are possible, then the wish, then the surrender to the will of God.[14] This prayer of Jesus is, as Daube points out, "the prayer of a Jew on his deathbed minus the confession of sin"; he makes the acknowledgment "expected of a Jew preparing for death." For me, the feature of the prayer that matters is the omission of the confession of sin. What religious Jew would omit this? Only, I suggest, one who is being portrayed as believing he is the Messiah.[15]

In Jerusalem, Jesus cleanses the Temple (Mark 11.15ff.). John's fuller version is a valuable correction to Mark. Whether or not John exaggerates the uncontrolled violence that it ascribes to Jesus, the specificity of the account demonstrates just how great was Jesus' outrage to institutionalized Judaism.[16]

> John 2.14. In the temple he found people selling cattle, sheep, and doves, and the money changers seated at their tables. 15. Making a whip of cords, he drove all of them out of the temple, both the sheep and the cattle. He also poured out the coins of the money changers and overturned their tables. 16. He told those who were selling the doves, "Take these things out of here! Stop making my Father's house a marketplace!"

John's designation of the victims of Jesus' rage is indisputably correct: money changers and sellers of cattle, sheep, and doves.

The two main standards of coinage that circulated in Jerusalem were the denarius and the didrachm. Both these pagan issues were unacceptable for the payment of the Temple tax. The basic denarius, for example, has on the obverse a bust of the emperor Tiberius, hence a graven image; and on the reverse his mother Livia representing the goddess Pax, even more offensive. The function of the money changers was to give Tyrian coinage in return for denarii and didrachms. They thus performed a service for the Temple and for all Jews, and their presence in the Temple precincts was expressly permitted and regulated by rabbinic law.[17] Paying the Temple tax was an important sign of Jewish identity: it marked one as a Jew.[18] Cattle, sheep, and doves were the sacrificial animals.[19] The sellers performed a very useful, indeed quasi-religious, function because pilgrims for Passover would otherwise have had considerable difficulties in finding ritually appropriate sacrifices.[20] The sale of doves for sacrifice at any time at the Temple was under the control of the temple authorities. The presence of cattle sellers in the Temple was lawful, as appears incidentally from Mishnah Shekalim 7.2.[21] Thus, Jesus committed a violent assault in the Temple, and he obstructed the payment of the Temple taxes and the performance of the Passover sacrifices. Just how outrageous his behavior was will become clearer when we remember that God (at Deuteronomy 12) had centralized worship and sacrifice to him at one place, and that place for the Jews (as opposed to the Samaritans) was the Temple at Jerusalem. Jesus' behavior was outrageous to the Pharisees, who were the most observant, to the Sadducees, who had control of the Temple, and indeed to all who paid the Temple tax and observed the Passover sacrifice.

This is Jesus' first confrontation with the Sadducees, and he has provoked it in a particularly public and hostile way. It is also the first time that Jesus has gone out of his way to anger ordinary Jews, though at times in the past he has clearly upset them.

It is not easy—I am tempted to say it is impossible—to understand why these quasi-religious and lawful activities in the Temple precincts drive Jesus to fury.[22] The obvious explanation of the apparently irrational event is that Jesus is deliberately provoking his own death. Certainly his death will be the obvious result.

In this regard the confrontation with the Sadducees is particularly noteworthy. Although, as we know from Josephus,[23] public esteem for them was limited, their political and social position was (virtually) unassailable, unless by someone who might be thought to be the Messiah. The chief priests were a hereditary class, and no one else could be included among the chief priests. Only they could offer sacrifice, and they were needed for the performance of every individual's religious obligations.[24] Jesus is willing his death.[25]

(Scholars often insist that a dispute between Jesus and the Pharisees over the Sabbath, purity, and food is unlikely to have led to his death. Thus E. P. Sanders says, "That judgment [i.e., that it did] is made in part on the assumption that the Pharisees rigidly controlled first-century Palestine and could enforce compliance with their interpretation of the law."[26] I disagree. First, Jesus also had to involve the Sadducees to achieve his death: the Pharisees had no overall control, and none need be suggested. Second, the Pharisees were not interested in enforcing compliance with their interpretation of the law. The issue was different: authority. And it was Jesus who provoked the confrontation.)

But Jesus is willing his death in a particular way: by stoning under the authority of the Sanhedrin. For this he needs to rouse the anger of the Sadducees, a fundamentally important constituent of that court. Indeed, a Sadducee was always president of the court. Until this point Jesus has deliberately angered only the Pharisees, but now he needs the wrath of the Sadducees. For Jesus his outrage in the Temple is a necessity.

Jesus is asked in the Temple by the chief priests, scribes, and elders the authority by which he does such things (Mark

11.27ff.), and in a roundabout way he refuses to answer, thus compounding his offense. It must be stressed that the chief priests and others have every justification to ask Jesus for the authority for his behavior. For Jesus to set the question at naught represents intolerable behavior. Jesus then begins to speak to them in parables (Mark 12.1ff.). The parable of the wicked tenants of the vineyard is more comprehensible than most of Jesus' teaching. Once it is understood that this has a disguised meaning—and such tales in disguise were common, as in the fables of Aesop—its point is plain and, as we are expressly told (Mark 12.12), it is told against those who questioned him, and they realize this.

The point of the parable must be grasped. The wicked tenants to whom the vineyard is leased are the chief priests, scribes, and elders. After the owner, who is God, is injured in the person of his slaves and still is not given his due, he sends his last dependent, his beloved son—Jesus, in fact—whom he believes they will respect. But they kill him, too. Jesus is telling those who question him that they will kill him. He is still confronting them, forcing them to take action. He also tells them the outcome, still in parable: God will destroy them and give the inheritance to others (Mark 12.9). They will lose their position as the chosen people.[27]

They want to arrest him, but they fear the crowd and go away (Mark 12.12). The Pharisees and Herodians then try to trap him with the question of paying taxes to the Romans (Mark 12.13ff.). Jesus disputes with them over bodily resurrection and the woman married successively to seven brothers (Mark 12.18ff.). Then:

Mark 12.28. One of the scribes came near and heard them disputing with one another, and seeing that he answered

them well, he asked him, "Which commandment is the first
of all?" 29. Jesus answered, "The first is, 'Hear, O Israel:
the Lord our God, the Lord is one; 30. you shall love the
Lord your God with all your heart, and with all your soul,
and with all your mind, and with all your strength.' 31.
The second is this, 'You shall love your neighbor as yourself.' There is no other commandment greater than these."
32. Then the scribe said to him, "You are right, Teacher;
you have truly said that 'he is one, and besides him there
is no other'; 33. and 'to love him with all the heart, and
with all the understanding, and with all the strength,' and
'to love one's neighbor as oneself'—this is much more important than all whole burnt offerings and sacrifices." 34.
When Jesus saw that he answered wisely, he said to him,
"You are not far from the kingdom of God." After that no
one dared to ask him any question.

This time, for once, Jesus gives clear religious and socially ori-
ented teaching. He then virtually reveals himself as the Messiah,
who would not be descended from David (Mark 12.35ff.). But
shortly thereafter he again gives way to vituperation:

Mark 12.38. As he taught, he said, "Beware of the scribes,
who like to walk around in long robes, and to be greeted
with respect in the marketplaces, 39. and to have the best
seats in the synagogues and places of honor at banquets!
40. They devour widows' houses and for the sake of appearance say long prayers. They will receive the greater
condemnation."

Jesus' behavior is very strange. He is asked by what authority
he does these things, that is, cleanses the Temple. The Pharisees and Sadducees put questions to him. He heaps abuse on the

scribes. But he has, in revolutionary fashion, just attacked the whole principle of the Temple. What were his follow-up plans? Time is passing. The answer is that Jesus had no follow-up plans except to incite the Jewish leaders to move against him. There is also a marked silence about the reaction of the people to his acts in the Temple. They are surely totally bewildered. They gave him a tumultuous welcome on his approach to Jerusalem. But then he disrupted the Passover. We are not told that the people helped him in his attack in the Temple precincts. Nor should we assume that they did. After all, those who were present would be the observing Jews who had come for the festival. Their reaction now will have been one of wait-and-see. It is on this basis that we can understand that after the tumultuous welcome, the leaders are afraid to arrest Jesus, but in the end the crowd abuses him on the cross.

Two days before the Passover the chief priests and scribes are seeking to arrest Jesus secretly and kill him, but not during the festival, in case the people riot (Mark 14.1f.). Judas goes to the chief priests to betray Jesus, and they promise him money (Mark 14.10f.).

Later, after the Passover dinner, Jesus goes with his disciples to Gethsemane (Mark 14.32). Judas arrives with a crowd carrying swords and clubs from the chief priests, scribes, and elders, and they arrest Jesus (Mark 14.43ff.). One who stood near drew his sword and cut off the ear of the high priest's slave. No significance should be attached to the fact that one who was near Jesus had a sword: Josephus tells us that even the Essenes carried weapons when they were traveling because they feared highway robbers, even though they carried nothing else.[28]

Mark 14.48. Then Jesus said to them, "Have you come out with swords and clubs to arrest me as though I were a bandit? 49. Day after day I was with you in the temple teaching, and you did not arrest me. But let the scriptures be fulfilled." 50. All of them deserted him and fled.

We know the answer to Jesus' question: they were afraid to arrest him publicly.

Very little attempt, if any, is made to capture the disciples, though one young man is caught by his sole garment, but he escapes, leaving it behind (Mark 14.51f.). Jesus is taken to the high priest, where the chief priests, scribes, and elders are assembled (Mark 14.53ff.). There is a trial before the Sanhedrin, and the court looks for testimony to put Jesus to death (Mark 14.55). The trial is illegal probably because it was held in a private house and certainly because it was held at night. The leaders are in a hurry, and they may still fear the crowd. Yet, despite this, the judges insist on the very stringent rules of evidence being adhered to. Many persons give false witness, but their testimony does not agree (Mark 14.56).[29] We are told expressly of only one accusation: "We heard him say, 'I will destroy this temple made with hands, and within three days I will build another not made with hands'" (Mark 14.58). That this accusation should be made is entirely plausible, and it could well have been made in good faith. It corresponds to a discussion with his disciples:

> Mark 13.1. As he came out of the temple, one of his disciples said to him, "Look, Teacher, what large stones and what large buildings!" 2. Then Jesus asked him, "Do you see these great buildings? Not one stone will be left here upon another; all will be thrown down."

One who overheard this could easily interpret Jesus as saying he would destroy the Temple. The episode also occurs in Matthew 24.1ff. and Luke 21.5ff., but that is scarcely further evidence. More important, it occurs also in John in a much more pointed way.

John 2.18. The Jews then said to him, "What sign can you show us for doing this?" 19. Jesus answered them, "Destroy this temple, and in three days I will raise it up." 20. The Jews then said, "This temple has been under construction for forty-six years, and will you raise it up in three days?" 21. But he was speaking of the temple of his body.

Thus, in John, Jesus is thought to be declaring that he will destroy the Temple. In both Mark and John the timing of the episode is the same: shortly after the cleansing of the Temple. It is reasonable to believe some such discussion did take place.[30] The accusation is plausible, especially after his outrage in the Temple. Mark 15.29 confirms that a major accusation against Jesus was that he had claimed he would destroy the Temple and rebuild it. Jesus is on the cross:

Those who passed by derided him, shaking their heads and saying, "Aha! You who would destroy the temple and build it in three days, 30. save yourself, and come down from the cross!"

The idea—that Jesus had claimed he would destroy the Temple —endured even in the later tradition. Thus, when Stephen was arrested and brought before the Sanhedrin:

Acts 6.13. They set up false witnesses who said, "This man never stops saying things against this holy place and the law; for we have heard him say that this Jesus of Nazareth will destroy this place and will change the customs that Moses handed on to us."

Still the judges will not convict Jesus. We may presume they believe that he had said he would destroy the Temple, but the required evidence of two witnesses agreeing on every point is lacking.

The high priest intervenes to break the impasse. He questions Jesus and asks if he is the Messiah, and Jesus admits it (Mark 14.61f.). The high priest then tears his clothes and asks what need there is of further witnesses because they have heard Jesus' blasphemy (Mark 14.63f.). This rending of garments is deliberately inappropriate. As described in the Mishnah, the judges should tear their garments, not when declaring the accused guilty, but the following morning when they have the required meeting to pronounce their sentence and they condemn the accused to death. And, moreover, the high priest is not allowed to tear his garments.[31] But the high priest's bullying tactic pays off. The judges all weakly give in and condemn Jesus as deserving death (Mark 14.64). The Sanhedrin reassembles the following morning (Mark 15.1), as required by law, and they hand Jesus over to the Roman governor, Pontius Pilate. Pilate asks Jesus if he is the king of the Jews, and Jesus gives no straight answer (Mark 15.2). Thus, Pilate is inquiring into a secular offense against the Romans. The chief priests accuse Jesus (Mark 15.3). The insistence of Pilate's inquiry into a possible secular crime, and the priests' accusations of this, rather than reporting their condemnation of Jesus, indicate that at the morning session the judges had regained their courage and had refused to condemn Jesus. If they had, they would have executed Jesus themselves, instead of handing him over to the Romans. Not only did the Sanhedrin have power to impose the death sentence, but often it carried it out.[32] The appropriate execution for his religious offenses was stoning by the Jews, not crucifixion by the Romans. Mark glosses over the Sanhedrin's failure to condemn because he does not want to emphasize the role of the Romans in Jesus' conviction. And, of course, the Sanhedrin, while accepting it lacked the necessary evidence for Jesus' condemnation, still wanted him to be put to death. The judges were absolutely sure of Jesus' guilt: they simply did not have the necessary technical evidence.[33]

(For judges to fail to convict a person they are sure is guilty because they observe very technical rules of evidence, more strictly than might seem appropriate in the circumstances, is not primitive, nor does it imply that the judges are unaware that the rules can fail them.[34] Rather, legal rules cannot always meet the variety of human life, and these particular rules were meant to protect a defendant and should not easily be neglected. In this instance, I suggest, the judges who voted for acquittal in the morning would be particularly aware of the nature of these rules of evidence. They had acquiesced in holding an illegal trial at night, yet they had insisted on following the evidentiary rules and had been browbeaten and outmaneuvered by the high priest. Now they were reaffirming their judicial standards; they would be confused and feeling guilty; they would want to redeem their past behavior while still believing Jesus to be a blasphemer. Nor should we see only cynicism in judges who, having failed to convict, hand over an accused to another court on a different charge: if you can't get him for murder, try tax evasion.)

Sherwin-White's treatment of the trial is instructive. He claims, "In Mark and Matthew, whose narratives cohere very closely, there is no doubt that the Sanhedrin passes sentence for blasphemy." But then he significantly adds, "Mark certainly gives no clear explanation of the connexion between the Sanhedrin session and the trial before Pilate."[35] Yes. Precisely therein lies the problem for explanations other than the one I am proposing.

The Crucifixion was a defeat for Jesus in more ways than the obvious. As I stressed at the beginning of this chapter, Jesus was uninterested in secular politics. But he had come to Jerusalem for the first time, to seek his death to fulfill a prophesy—but not at the hands of the Romans. So long as he was in Galilee, he was beyond the jurisdiction of the Sanhedrin. But he came to Jerusalem and disrupted the Passover preparations at the Temple, the one place where, for the Jews, God permitted sacrifice. Matthew and Luke are helpful here. Jesus declaimed:

Matthew 23.29. "Woe to you, scribes and Pharisees, hypocrites! For you build the tombs of the prophets and decorate the graves of the righteous, 30. and you say, 'If we had lived in the days of our ancestors, we would not have taken part with them in shedding the blood of the prophets.' 31. Thus you testify against yourselves that you are descendants of those who murdered the prophets. 32. Fill up, then, the measure of your ancestors. 33. You snakes, you brood of vipers! How can you escape being sentenced to hell? 34. Therefore I send you prophets, sages, and scribes, some of whom you will kill and crucify, and some you will flog in your synagogues and pursue from town to town, 35. so that upon you may come all the righteous blood shed on earth, from the blood of righteous Abel to the blood of Zechariah son of Barachiah, whom you murdered between the sanctuary and the altar. 36. Truly I tell you, all this will come upon this generation.

37. "Jerusalem, Jerusalem, the city that kills the prophets and stones those who are sent to it! How often have I desired to gather your children together as a hen gathers her brood under her wings, and you were not willing! 38. See, your house is left to you, desolate. 39. For I tell you, you will not see me again until you say, 'Blessed is the one who comes in the name of the Lord.'"

Luke 13.31. At that very hour some Pharisees came and said to him, "Get away from here, for Herod wants to kill you." 32. He said to them, "Go and tell that fox for me, 'Listen, I am casting out demons and performing cures today and tomorrow, and on the third day I finish my work. 33. Yet today, tomorrow, and the next day I must be on my way, because it is impossible for a prophet to be killed outside of Jerusalem.' 34. Jerusalem, Jerusalem, the city that kills the prophets and stones those who are sent to it! How often have I desired to gather your children together as a hen gathers her brood under her wings, and you were not willing! 35. See, your house is left to you. And I tell you, you will not see me until the time comes when you say, 'Blessed is the one who comes in the name of the Lord.' "

In the two Gospels the words are spoken at very different points of time, yet they clearly go back to the same tradition, one not recorded by Mark.

The precision of Matthew 23.37 is particularly striking: "Jerusalem, Jerusalem, the city that kills the prophets and stones those who are sent to it." Jesus is referring to himself, inter alios. Thus, "For I tell you, you will not see me again until you say, 'Blessed is the one who comes in the name of the Lord'" (Matthew 23.39). Jesus expects, even wants, to be killed at Jerusalem—the city that kills the prophets—and that by stoning. He wants the Sanhedrin to execute him. It should be emphasized that here, in his goading, he is again concentrating on the Pharisees rather than the Sadducees. In Matthew the episode is placed reasonably enough after the cleansing of the Temple.

The episode is recounted in Luke in a rather less convincing way. Jesus was only on his way to Jerusalem (Luke 13.22), but he was warned by Pharisees to get away from there because Herod wanted to kill him (Luke 13.31). Perhaps Jesus was still in Galilee; perhaps Herod was already in Jerusalem (Luke 23.7). But what really matters for us are Jesus' words: "and the next day I must be on my way, because it is impossible for a prophet

to be killed outside of Jerusalem. Jerusalem, Jerusalem, the city
that kills the prophets and stones those who are sent to it!" (Luke
13.33f.). Thus, even more clearly than in Matthew the tradition
is that Jesus went to Jerusalem to be killed, at that as a prophet,
and by stoning, thus by the Sanhedrin.[36]

In Mark, Jesus prophesies three times that he will be put to
death (8.31, 9.31, 10.32f.). In the most specific (Mark 10.32f.)
the prediction is that the chief priests and scribes will condemn
him to death, and they will hand him over to the Gentiles, who
will execute him. This is, of course, written with hindsight: the
Romans did crucify Jesus. The other two less specific predictions
better reveal Jesus' mindset, as has long been realized. In Mark
8.31, "he will be rejected by the elders, the chief priests, and the
scribes and be killed." In Mark 9.31, he "is to be betrayed into
human hands and they will kill him." Long ago Rudolf Otto,
writing specifically of Mark 9.31, stressed, "He thinks that he
will fall into the hands of excited fanatics. And it is just as indu-
bitable that he was not thinking of crucifixion, but of stoning by
a popular mob."[37] So long as one (mistakenly) believes the Sanhedrin could not execute a death sentence, one cannot believe
Jesus expected to be put to death by that court but by a mob. But
indubitably Jesus did not expect to be crucified by the Romans.

The Sanhedrin found Jesus guilty at the first stage of the trial,
but at the second stage the following morning they did not convict. It is not clear whether this was because after reconsideration
they were more conscious of the flaws of the trial or because
some were still afraid of the wrath of the crowd. The Sanhedrin
brought Jesus before Pilate who, after a summary trial, found
him guilty of sedition (Mark 15.26). But Pilate was unwilling
to execute him probably primarily because he also was hesitant
about incurring the wrath of the crowd and starting a riot. He
offered to release Jesus, but the crowd demanded that Barabbas

be freed instead. Once Pilate knew that the people would not riot if he executed Jesus, he had no reason to spare him. So he ordered his crucifixion.

Thus, at the end, Jesus lost everything. The Sanhedrin did not sentence him to death. Instead he suffered what was for him a meaningless execution by crucifixion at the hands of the Romans, for whom he cared nothing. It is partly on this account that we have the efforts in the Gospels to highlight the responsibility of the Jews for Jesus' death, even to the point of having Pilate desire to hand Jesus over to them for crucifixion.

The execution showed him he was not the Messiah. It is on this basis, and only on this basis, that we can make sense of Mark 15.34:

> At three o'clock Jesus cried out with a loud voice, "Eloi, Eloi, lama sabacthani?" which means "My God, My God, why have you forsaken me?"[38]

✛

APPENDIX

✛ ✛ ✛

IN THE CONCLUDING CHAPTER I SET OUT MY SCENARIO
of the events leading up to the Crucifixion of Jesus. That scenario was
based largely on a close reading of Mark and is, I hope, faithful to the
Gospel texts and plausible both psychologically and historically. But
I should like to bring forward two other possible approaches to Mark
really so that they might be rejected.

First, it might be suggested that Mark's version of the trial contains
so many errors of procedure—the meeting at night, the high priest
rending his garments and, at that, at the wrong time—that no credence
can be given to any part of the account, including the meeting on the
following morning. But such an approach would ignore the tight structure of Mark in general—witness the relationship of the confrontations
in chapter 2 and the beginning of chapter 3—and the Jewishness of the
structure in particular—witness the belief that Jesus was insane being
linked with his relatives looking for him, the triple structure of Jesus'
prayer at Gethsemane, Peter's three denials, and the four questions
after the cleansing of the Temple, where the question on contradictions makes sense in Mark but not in the other Synoptics. It should be
admitted that Mark knows what it is about.

The second suggestion would be the diametrically opposite, that

Mark is so concerned with structure that it massages it—thus, we do not know that Peter's denials occurred in the order recounted, and limiting the questions after the cleansing of the Temple to precisely the four seems artificial. But even if we concede that Jesus' trial has perhaps been managed to increase the drama, that would in no way indicate that a formal sentence of death imposed on Jesus by the Sanhedrin on the following morning has been cut out. Such an excision would, in fact, have served only to reduce the dramatic tension. It should also be emphasized that if Mark and its sources were composed in societies where Christians were of Jewish origin and still not fully separated from other Jews, that would be no reason for its reducing emphasis on any guilt of particular Jewish leaders. Thus, I suggest we should still accept Mark 15.1–2 at face value.

On the morning after the illegal trial, the Sanhedrin did meet, but it uttered no conviction of Jesus for a religious crime and did not sentence him to death. Instead, the council delivered Jesus to Pontius Pilate, who tried him for a secular crime against the Romans. To read into Mark 15.1 a conviction and sentence of death by the Sanhedrin that are not mentioned, that are then not followed by the appropriate carrying out of the sentence but are followed by a Roman secular trial at the instigation of the Sanhedrin for a very different crime, makes no sense. Such an approach could attain some degree of plausibility only if one could admit, as I cannot, that John 18.31 provides strong evidence that the Sanhedrin could not put a Jew to death. It is well to recall here the treatment of any trial and sentence by the Sanhedrin in the other Gospels. In John there is simply no trial of Jesus by the Sanhedrin. In Matthew nothing is said about a conviction and sentence of death on the following morning. Instead, Matthew 27.1 records that the Sanhedrin "took counsel against Jesus to put him to death." To me, these words suggest some purpose other than carrying out a legally imposed death sentence.

My conclusion that a sentence of death was envisaged by the evangelist is purely a deduction from the repentance of Judas in Matthew 27.2ff. But the passing of a death sentence is not stated (and, I believe, did not exist in the basic tradition used by Matthew). Luke, in its turn, is confused. There was only one session, in the morning, at which the Sanhedrin does seem to have found Jesus guilty of blasphemy (Luke 22.66ff.) But then they took Jesus to Pilate, saying they had found Jesus had committed a religious crime and two secular crimes (Luke 23.1ff.). Then there is the strange testimony of Luke 13.19:

> 19. He [the risen Jesus] asked them, "What things?" They replied, "The things about Jesus of Nazareth, who was a prophet mighty in deed and word before God and all the people, 20. and how our chief priests and leaders handed him over to be condemned to death and crucified him.

According to these texts the chief priests handed Jesus over to be condemned to death, so presumably for Luke here, the Sanhedrin had not condemned him. Even if one could accept that equal weight should be given to all four Gospels with regard to historical accuracy, and even if one could accept that the Sanhedrin did not have the power to carry out the death sentence, it would still be the case that we have remarkably little indirect, and no direct, evidence that at the legally required second trial session the Sanhedrin found Jesus guilty of a religious crime. The account in Mark, complete with its trial illegalities, makes a psychological sense that is lacking in Matthew and Luke.

✠

ABBREVIATIONS

✠ ✠ ✠

Albright and Mann, *Matthew*   W. F. Albright and C. S. Mann, *Matthew* (New York, 1971).

Bammel, *Trial*   Ernst Bammel, *The Trial of Jesus* (Naperville, Ill., 1970).

Brown, *Death*, 1, 2   Raymond E. Brown, *The Death of the Messiah*, 2 vols. (New York, 1994).

Cranfield, *Mark*   C. E. B. Cranfield, *The Gospel according to Saint Mark* (Cambridge, 1972).

Daube, *Civil Disobedience*   David Daube, *Civil Disobedience in Antiquity* (Edinburgh, 1972).

Daube, *New Testament*   *The New Testament and Rabbinic Judaism* (London, 1956).

Fitzmyer, *Luke I–IX*   Joseph A. Fitzmyer, *The Gospel according to Luke I–IX* (Garden City, 1981).

Fitzmyer, *Luke X–XXIV*	Joseph A. Fitzmyer, *The Gospel according to Luke X–XXIV* (Garden City, N.Y., 1985).
Grant, *Historical Introduction*	Robert Grant, *A Historical Introduction to the New Testament* (London, 1963).
Jeremias, *Eucharistic Words*	Joachim Jeremias, *The Eucharistic Words of Jesus*, 3d ed., trans. N. Perrin (New York, 1966).
Mann, *Mark*	C. S. Mann, *Mark* (Garden City, N.Y., 1986).
Mishnah	*The Mishnah*, trans. Herbert Danby (Oxford, 1933).
Sanders, *Jewish Law*	E. P. Sanders, *Jewish Law from Jesus to the Mishnah* (Philadelphia, 1990).
Schürer, *History*, 2	Emil Schürer, *The History of the Jewish People in the Age of Jesus Christ* (175 B.C.–A.D. 135), vol. 2, 2nd ed., ed. Geza Vermes, Fergus Millar, Matthew Black, Martin Goodmar, and Pamela Vermes (Edinburgh, 1979).
Sherwin-White, *Roman Society*	A. N. Sherwin-White, *Roman Society and Roman Law in the New Testament* (Oxford, 1963).
Strack-Billerbeck, *Kommentar*, 1, 2	Hermann L. Strack and Paul Billerbeck, *Kommentar zum Neuen Testament aus Talmud und Midrasch*, vol. 1, 5th ed. (Munich, 1969); vol. 2, 4th ed. (Munich, 1965).

Taylor, *Mark*

Vincent Taylor, *The Gospel according to St. Mark* (London, 1953).

Watson, *Jesus and the Jews*

Alan Watson, *Jesus and the Jews: The Pharisaic Tradition in John* (Athens, Ga., 1995).

Winter, *Trial*

Paul Winter, *On the Trial of Jesus* (Berlin, 1961).

✠

NOTES

✠ ✠ ✠

PREFACE

1. Two very recent contributions of the "What must have been" school are, Simon Légasse, *Le procès de Jésus* 1. *L'histoire* (Paris, 1994); Enoch Powell, *The Evolution of the Gospel: A New Translation of the First Gospel* (New Haven, 1994).

1 THE HISTORICAL BACKGROUND

1. In this section I essentially follow Schürer, *History*, 2:488ff.; see also Brown, *Death*, 1:473ff.

2. On Malachi see, for example, A. E. Hill in *The Anchor Bible Dictionary* (New York, 1992), 4:478ff.

3. Cf. Matthew 11.11ff.; Mark 9.11ff.

4. Matthew 16.14; Mark 6.15, 8.28; Luke 9.8, 9.19; John 1.21.

5. Cf. Schürer, *History*, 2:503; Marinus de Jonge, ed., *Outside the Old Testament* (New York, 1985), 160f. The translation here is that of de Jonge.

6. J. J. Collins in *The Old Testament Pseudepigrapha*, ed. James H.

Charlesworth (Garden City, N.Y., 1983), 1:355. Schürer suggests a date around 140 B.C.: *History*, 2:501. The translation here is that of Collins.

7. The Book of Jubilees should also be mentioned in this context. 31.18. Then he [Isaac] spoke to Judah: "May the Lord give you strength and power to trample on all who hate you. Be a ruler— you and one of your sons—for Jacob's children."

"And one of your sons" is regarded as pointing to a future Messiah: Schürer, *History*, 2:507. The work was probably written between 160 and 150 B.C.: cf. J. C. VanderKam in de Jonge, *Outside the Old Testament*, 115.

8. Cf. Schürer, *History*, 2:530f.

9. See, in general, Emil Schürer, *The History of the Jewish People in the Age of Jesus Christ*, 2d ed., eds. G. Vermes and F. Miller (Edinburgh, 1973), 1:243ff.

10. See, in general, Abraham Schalit, *König Herodes* (Berlin, 1969).

11. Josephus *Jewish War* 1.608.

12. Ibid., 1.669.

13. Ibid., 2.4ff.

14. See, for example, Schürer, *History*, 2:600.

15. Josephus *Jewish War* 2.94ff.

16. Josephus *Jewish Antiquities* 17.342ff., 17.354f.

17. See, for example, Harold W. Hoehner, *Herod Antipas* (Cambridge, 1972).

18. Josephus *Jewish Antiquities* 15.403ff., 18.90ff., 20.6f.

19. Ibid., 15.403–6.

20. Cf., for example, Winter, *Trial*, 16f.

21. Josephus *Jewish Antiquities* 17.355.

22. Ibid., 18.2–5.

23. Ibid., 18.9ff.

24. *Jewish War* 2.118; cf. 2.433.

25. For a general discussion see Brown, *Death*, 1:686ff.

26. *Jewish Antiquities* 18.118.

27. For a nuanced view of the pharisaic attitude to oral law see Sanders, *Jewish Law*, 97ff. The view of oral law that I am putting for-

ward is that of a historian. Believing Jews, even present-day Jews, have a different image, that of the "Dual Torah" the written law and the oral law, in which the former has no primacy. On this approach, God's original revelation was of both the written law and the oral law in its entirety which has been passed down intact through the ages: see for example, Babylonian Talmud, B'rakot, 4b. A good account of this is by Perry Dane, "The Oral Law and the Jurisprudence of a Textless Text," *S'vara* 2 (1991): 11ff.

28. For this see Danby, *Mishnah*, 795.

29. On tithes see, for example, Sanders, *Jewish Law*, 43ff.

30. For the Pharisees see, for example, Schürer, *History*, 2:388ff.

31. Cf., for example, Sanders, *Jewish Law*, 6ff., 35ff., 40.

32. But the Sadducees had their own interpretations of the written law: see, for example, Mishnah Makkoth 1.6; Mishnah Yadaim 4.6f. We do not know how authoritative they regarded such interpretations. In fact we know so little about the Sadducean view of law—if it was unitary—that we cannot really tell how far they diverged from the Pharisees.

33. For priests and Sadducees see, for example, Schürer, *History*, 2:227ff., 2:404ff.

34. Cf., for example, Geza Vermes, *Jesus the Jew* (London, 1973), 52ff.

35. The prevalence of magic in the hellenistic world is well brought out in the short account by Peter Green, *Alexander to Actium* (Berkeley, 1990), 597ff. For a bibliography for the ancient Near East see *The Anchor Bible Dictionary*, 4:466ff.; for Greece and Rome, *Der Kleine Pauly* (Munich, 1975), 5:1471f.

36. Tacitus *Historiae* 4.81; Dio *Roman History* 65.8.

2 ARREST, TRIAL, EXECUTION: MARK

1. Thus in John, Jesus' disciples ask who had sinned, the man born blind or his parents (9.2). The Pharisees say the man was born in sin (9.34).

2. Cf., for example, Cranfield, *Mark*, 98; Taylor, *Mark*, 195; Fitz-myer, *Luke, I–IX*, 583ff.

3. See infra, chapter 8.

4. Cf., for example, Taylor, *Mark*, 200f.

5. For the scope of *sinner* in the Gospels see, for example, Joachim Jeremias, *The Parables of Jesus*, 8th ed., trans. S. H. Hooke (London, 1972), 124ff.

6. Mark 14.3; Luke 7.36–37, 7.49, 11.37, 14.15. For many other references see Joachim Jeremias, *The Eucharistic Words of Jesus*, 3d ed., trans. N. Perrin (New York, 1966), 48. See also Robert G. Bratcher and Eugene A. Nida, *A Translator's Handbook on the Gospel of Mark* (New York, 1981), 85.

7. Cf., for example, Sanders, *Jewish Law*, 81ff. David Daube has noted, "It is arguable that, as originally conceived at least, the question implies little criticism, rather mostly curiosity—though we must remember that any deviance from the customary is apt to make people uncomfortable": "Responsibilities of Master and Disciples in the Gospels," *New Testament Studies* 19 (1972): 4.

8. Cranfield says of the question about fasting: "Luke connects this closely with the preceding [i.e., episode]: but Mark, probably rightly, makes no such connection": *Mark*, 107. For me, in Mark the two episodes, together with the next, are very closely connected in thought.

9. Mishnah Shabbath 7.2. See, for example, Strack-Billerbeck, *Kommentar* 1:241ff.

10. Daube, "Master and Disciples," 4f.; Daube, *New Testament*, 67ff.; cf. Schürer, *History*, 2:334ff.

11. Again, Cranfield believes this is not linked with the preceding episodes; *Mark*, 114. I disagree.

12. Perhaps surprisingly Cranfield terms this "the last of the group of conflict-stories": *Mark*, 118.

13. See, for example, Taylor, *Mark*, 224; Phillip Carrington, *According to Mark* (Cambridge, 1960), 73.

14. A typical expression is that of Mann that Mark is not at first glance impressive: *Mark*, 77. He seems to be quite unaware of the

tightness of structure. On the tendency to play down Mark see now David Daube, "Judas," *Rechtshistorisches Journal* 13 (1994): 21f.

15. Leviticus 14.1–32

16. Cf., for example, Sanders, *Jewish Law*, 1.

17. Cf. Daube, *Civil Disobedience*, 46.

18. See, for example, Taylor, *Mark*, 338f.; Cranfield, *Mark*, 232f.

19. Cf. Cranfield, *Mark*, 236.

20. On Corban see, for example, Taylor, *Mark*, 341f.; Cranfield, *Mark*, 237ff.

21. See Daube, *New Testament*, 170ff.

22. I will say nothing here about 7.14–23. The public pronouncement is unclear, and only in private does he explain it to the disciples: see Daube, *New Testament*, 141ff.

23. Sanders, for example, accepts Jesus as a charismatic figure: *Jewish Law*, 3. But, he says, "a charismatic does not set out to take a stance on a series of legal questions, though he may bump up against them now and then. It is in theory possible that a charismatic might stumble into serious questions about the law, and into quite serious offences against it, though I know of no evidence that this happened in Jesus' case." But here the charismatic authority, Jesus, deliberately confronts the institutional authority, the Pharisees, who take their stance on the law. The issue is not Jesus' breaking of the law, but his challenge to Pharisaic authority. It is important to remember the episodes in Mark 2 where the Pharisees did not accuse Jesus.

24. See, for example, Strack-Billerbeck, *Kommentar*, 1:845; Taylor, *Gospel*, 456; Albright and Mann take Hosanna in its original meaning, not as a cry of praise: *Matthew*, 252.

25. This approach was not strictly observed: see the instances in Strack-Billerbeck, *Kommentar*, 2:26.

26. In a letter to me Steven F. Friedell produces a different perspective: "I had always thought that the word was a compound of two Hebrew words—*Hosha, Na*—not an Aramaic word. The Hoshana is a regular part of the synagogue service during Sukkot. One marches around the Torah carrying and waving the Lulav reciting verses and

ending each with "Hoshana." On Hoshana Rabba, the seventh day of
Sukkot, one marches seven times around the Torah. At some point
in Jewish history it was believed that the Messiah might come during
Sukkot. Some of the Haftorah's that are read during the festival discuss the coming of the end of days and the Messiah. (On the first day
of Sukkot the reading is from Zechariah 14, and on the intermediate
Sabbath the reading is from Ezekiel 38.18–39.16 concerning God and
Magog.) Also, inserted into the grace after meals during Sukkot is a
plea that God rebuild the Tabernacle of David which has fallen." Friedell also observes that *hosha* in Hebrew appears in Jeremiah 31.6 and
Psalms 86.2; *na* in Hebrew appears frequently, for instance in Genesis
12.11–13.

27. The contrary is often held: see the discussion in Taylor, *Mark*,
451ff. Cranfield talks of "the most notable restraint regarding messianic colour": *Mark*, 347; cf. 352ff.

28. Mishnah Shekalim 7.2.

29. Ibid., 1.3.

30. Ibid., 6.5.

31. Cf., for example, Taylor, *Mark*, 468f.

32. On this see Daube, *New Testament*, 151ff., 217ff.

33. See, for example, John Martin Creed, *The Gospel according to St.
Luke* (London, 1930), 243; Fitzmyer, *Luke X–XXIV*, 127ff.

34. Cranfield, among others, offers a very sophisticated interpretation: *Mark*, 372: "Though the obligation to pay to Caesar some of
his own coinage in return for the amenities his rule provided is af-
firmed, the idolatrous claims expressed on the coins are rejected. God's
rights are to be honoured. Here Jesus is not saying that there are two
quite separate independent spheres, that of Caesar and that of God (for
Caesar and all that is his belong to God); but he is indicating that there
are obligations to Caesar which do not infringe the rights of God but
are indeed ordained by God." For a good discussion of views that have
been held see Fitzmyer, *Luke X–XXIV*, 1289ff.

35. I am leaving aside at this stage Jesus' subsequent statement that
the Messiah is not the son of David (12.35ff.). See chapter 12.

36. Cf. Brown, *Death*, 1:247.

37. Ibid., 294ff.

38. Ibid., 433f.

39. Mishnah Sanhedrin 11.2.

40. Ibid., 4.1.

41. On this see Daube, "Judas," in *RJ*, 21.

42. This statement is made despite Mishnah Sanhedrin 7.5.

43. Cf. Leviticus 10.6f.

44. Cf. Brown, *Death*, 1:679ff.

45. It is, of course, possible that Simon acquired the nickname before he became a disciple of Jesus. Then at the least the nickname would tell us nothing about Jesus' attitude to Zealots, but its very retention would still suggest that Jesus' disciples were no revolutionaries.

46. Cf., for example, D. Cohen and C. Paulus, "Einige Bemerkungen zum Prozess Jesu bei den Synoptikern," *Zeitschrift der Savigny-Stiftung (romanistische Abteilung)* 102 (1985): 445f.

47. The hesitations sometimes expressed, for example, by Brown, *Death*, 1:710ff., of the nature of the trial by Pontius Pilate are quite unfounded. It must be remembered that Jesus was not a Roman citizen. For a clear account of the powers of trial and execution of governors such as Pilate, see A. N. Sherwin-White, *Roman Society*, 1ff., 24ff.

48. *Epistulae* 10.96.

49. I believe it was, following G. E. M. de Ste. Croix, "Why Were the Early Christians Persecuted?" *Past and Present* 26 (1963): 6ff.; "Why Were the Early Christians Persecuted?—a Rejoinder," *Past and Present* 27 (1964): 28ff.

50. See, for example, A. N. Sherwin-White, *Oxford Classical Dictionary*, 2d ed. (Oxford, 1970), 846f.

3 ARREST, TRIAL, EXECUTION: JOHN

1. Cf. Daube, *Civil Disobedience*, 101ff.

2. See, for example, Deuteronomy 17.1.

3. Mishnah Shekalim 6.5; cf. Strack-Billerbeck, *Kommentar*, 1:850.

4. For the detailed argument on this see Watson, *Jesus and the Jews*, 80ff.

5. Sherwin-White, *Roman Society*, 32.

4 MATTHEW AND LUKE

1. Albright and Mann correctly point out that Jesus' behavior is a challenge and involves the issue of the authority of the Messiah in action: *Matthew*, 103. But the challenge in Mark is much stronger.

2. See Brown, *Death*, 1:389.

3. Strack and Billerbeck take the high priest's words as putting Jesus on oath: *Kommentar*, 1:1005f.; but see David Daube, "Judas," in *RJ*, 20f.

4. Cf. David Daube, "Judas," *California Law Review* 82 (1994): 95ff.

5. Mishnah Makkoth 1.6 records a dispute between the Sadducees and the Sages (i.e., Pharisees). The Sadducees held that a perjurer could be put to death only after the person falsely accused had been executed. The Sages' view was that a perjurer could be put to death after the judges heard his false testimony but only before the convicted person was executed. Deuteronomy 19.18 clearly supports the stance of the Sages, and this will be the older view: cf. David Daube, *Studies in Biblical Law* (Cambridge, 1947), 129.

The legal issue is enormously complicated. Judas' wicked behavior was not obviously the bearing of false evidence but betraying a fellow-Jew to hostile authorities and ultimately to an occupying foreign power. This is an act equally justifying the death penalty. For us, what really matters in this context is not the precise nature of Judas' offense but that Matthew 27.3 expressly tells us that it was because Jesus was condemned that Judas brought back the thirty pieces of silver and hanged himself.

6. Fitzmyer brings out well the dependence of these three episodes on Mark: *Luke I–IX*, 577ff., 586ff., 604ff.

7. Mishnah Sanhedrin 7.4. Mishnah Sanhedrin 8.1 indicates that Jesus would have been too old to be convicted of this offense (if it were ever punished), but the Mishnah often presents a later and idealized version of the law.

8. In fact, the meal was a banquet given in honor of Jesus: Jeremias, *Parables of Jesus*, 126.

9. See, for example, Fitzmyer, *Luke X–XXIV*, 942ff.

10. Ibid., 1010ff. and 1028ff.

11. Cf. ibid., 1038ff.

12. See Brown, *Death*, 1:389f.

13. For Jesus' "You say so," see Daube, "Judas," in *RJ*, 23.

14. Pilate certainly had jurisdiction. On *forum delicti* or *forum domicilii* see Sherwin-White, *Roman Society*, 28ff. For other explanations of Pilate's behavior see Fitzmyer, *Luke X–XXIV*, 1478ff.

15. Cf., for example, Cohen and Paulus, "Einige Bemerkungen zum Prozess Jesu bei den Synoptikern," 448ff.

5 MARK: MATTHEW AND LUKE

1. See, for example, Grant, *Historical Introduction*, 117f.; W. D. Davies, *Invitation to the New Testament* (Garden City, N.Y., 1966), 84ff.; specifically on Luke see Fitzmyer, *Luke I–IX*, 66ff.

2. Cf. Brown, *Death*, 1:803ff.

3. Cf. ibid., 1:760ff.

4. Daube, *Civil Disobedience*, 112ff. See the sources Daube cites.

5. For a different perspective by a scholar apparently unaware of Daube's analysis, see the detailed account in Brown, *Death*, 1:589ff. For the differences in the telling of Jesus' interaction with the Pharisees in Mark 2 and the corresponding passages in Matthew and Luke, I would add a further partial explanation. With the passage of time Christian tradition had come more to believe in the Pharisees as the "bad guys," with a corresponding inability to see that for a time their main interest was to find out what Jesus was like, not to persecute him.

6. For a concise account of differences in the extent of anti-Judaism in the Gospel accounts of the trial, see Brown, *Death*, 1:386ff.

7. Fitzmyer sees real political character in this accusation; perverting the nation, he says, is specifically obstructing the payment of taxes to Caesar and claiming to be an anointed king: *Luke X–XXIV*, 1473. This is unconvincing. The charge that Jesus claimed to be a king is a separate accusation: even there it is a subordinate charge. And why not simply and specifically claim he was obstructing the payment of taxes?

6 MARK AND JOHN

1. Much of this chapter is taken from my book *Jesus and the Jews*.

2. Cf. Daube, *Civil Disobedience*, 102.

3. On the translation and theological meaning see Raymond E. Brown, *The Gospel according to John: XIII–XXI* (Anchor Bible, Garden City, N.Y., 1970), 549f.

4. Ibid., 556.

5. Jeremias, *Eucharistic Words*, 41ff.; cf. Harold Riley, *The Making of Mark: An Exploration* (Macon, Ga., 1989), 228ff.

6. But I wish to stress that the evidence for the timing in John being inaccurate is independent of my claims about S.

7. See, for example, Julius Wellhausen, *Das Evangelium Johannis* (Berlin, 1908), 60; Jeremias, *Eucharistic Words*, 82.

8. Jeremias, *Eucharistic Words*, 49.

9. Jerusalem Talmud, Pesahim 10.1.37b: "R. Levi has said 'because slaves eat standing, here [at the Passover meal] people should recline to eat, to signify that they have passed from slavery to freedom.'" R. Levi was active around 300.

10. See, for example, Mark 14.3; Luke 7.36–37, 7.49, 11.37, 14.15. For many other references see Jeremias, *Eucharistic Words*, 48.

11. Jeremias, *Eucharistic Words*, 49. Mishnah Pesahim 10.1; Tosefta Pesahim 10.1; the translation of the former text is inaccurate in Danby, *Mishnah*, 150. The treatment by C. K. Barrett, *The Gospel according*

to St. John (Philadelphia, 1978), 441, of washing is informative and useful, but he seems to miss the point of religious purity. Raymond E. Brown is skeptical of Jeremias's claim that the disciples were levitically pure: *John: XIII–XXI*, 567.

12. If my overall argument is correct, and S shows Jesus as hostile to Jewish ritual, then John 13.10 (and presumably the surrounding verses) does not derive from S.

13. David Daube, *He That Cometh* (St. Paul's Lecture, London, 1966), 13.

14. Ibid., 6ff. Daube had a forerunner in Robert Eisler, "Das letzte Abendmahl," *Zeitschrift für die Neutestamentliche Wissenschaft* 24 (1925): 161ff. Cf. D. B. Carmichael, "David Daube on the Eucharist and the Passover Seder," *Journal for the Study of the New Testament* 42 (1991): 45ff.

15. For Robin Lane Fox it is John who has the timing right: *The Unauthorized Version: Truth and Fiction in the Bible* (New York, 1992), 294f. His main argument seems to be that "it rests on a primary source": cf. his 204ff.

16. Raymond E. Brown, *The Gospel according to John: I–XII* (Anchor Bible, New York, 1966), 429.

17. For Barrett, 11.45–54 "no doubt comes from John's pen": *St. John*, 404.

18. See Schürer, *History*, 2:212f.

19. Brown, *John: I–XII*, 439.

20. Cf. W. F. Howard, in *The Interpreter's Bible* (New York, 1952), 8:651; Barrett, *St. John*, 406.

21. The Greek "λῃσταί" (brigands: Matthew 27.38; Mark 15.27) is a term used by Josephus to designate those who took up arms against the Romans; *Jewish War* 2.228, 2.253, 2.254, 2.271, 4.198; *Jewish Antiquities* 20.161.

22. Cf., for example, E. Mary Smallwood, *The Jews under Roman Rule: From Pompey to Diocletian* (Leiden, 1976), 164.

23. *Jewish Antiquities* 18.116–19.

24. Matthew 3.11f.; Mark 1.7f.; Luke 3.15–17; John 1.19–27.

7 MARK AND JESUS' MINISTRY

1. Leviticus 14.2ff.
2. Cf. Taylor, *Mark*, 187; Cranfield, *Mark*, 92.
3. Leviticus 13.45.
4. Leviticus 14.34ff.
5. This need not mean that the leper recognized that Jesus was more than human: cf. Cranfield, *Mark*, 81.
6. This is to reject the rather pleasing conclusion expressed in Cranfield, *Mark*, 107: "The point of the whole verse may be summed up: For Jesus to refuse to have dealings with the disreputable would be as absurd as for a doctor to refuse to have to do with the sick; he has come on purpose to call sinners, and the disreputable people he is associating with are obvious members of that class." This implies that Jesus' call was also to the righteous, which is denied in the Gospel.
7. On secrecy in Mark, cf. for example, Grant, *Historical Introduction*, 121f.
8. The episode is also in Luke 9.49f.

8 THE SANHEDRIN

1. For the Sanhedrin in general see Schürer, *History*, 2:199ff.; Brown, *Death*, 1:339ff.
2. Josephus *Jewish Antiquities* 12.138.
3. See Schürer, *History*, 2:203 and n.7.
4. Josephus *Jewish Antiquities* 20.244.
5. Josephus *Jewish War* 1.170; *Jewish Antiquities* 14.91.
6. *Jewish Antiquities* 14.165ff.
7. Ibid., 14.175.
8. Ibid., 15.5.
9. Exodus 28f.; Leviticus 8–10; Numbers 16–18; cf. Schürer, *History*, 2:238ff.
10. *Jewish Antiquities* 18:16f.

11. But see Brown, *Death*, 1:350ff.

12. For a perplexed discussion see Brown, *Death*, 1:404ff.

13. See Watson, *Jesus and the Jews*, 103f.

14. Even the most sophisticated scholars forget at the times that John is a composite. It is that which explains much of the perplexity in Brown, *Death*, 1:405.

15. For a very different version of what follows, see, for example, Sherwin-White, *Roman Society*, 35ff.

16. For example, 1.4.

17. For example, 4.1.

18. For example, 4.5.

19. For example, 6.1ff.; 7.1ff.

20. For example, 6.3f.; 9.1.

21. For example, 7.5ff.; 8.1ff.; 9.1f.

22. Leviticus 24.14.

23. Joshua 7.19.

24. Joshua 7.25.

25. Deuteronomy 17.7.

26. Deuteronomy 21.23.

27. Cf. Smallwood, *Jews under Roman Rule*, 149.

28. Cf. Josephus *Jewish War* 5.194; *Jewish Antiquities* 15.417; Acts 21.28. See also Winter, *Trial*, 155 n.27.

29. Brown, *Death*, 1:366.

30. *Jewish Antiquities* 18:63f.

31. Cf. Winter, *Trial*, 18.

32. Josephus *Jewish Antiquities* 15.403ff.

33. Winter seems to accept that there was a judicial execution: *Trial*, 76, 192 n.3. He also lays stress, as I would not on the treatment of Paul from Acts 21.27 onwards: ibid., 76ff.

34. Daube correctly observes that in such circumstances the executions would be discreet: *New Testament*, 306f.

35. J. E. Allen suggests as a possibility from John 18.31 that the Jews failed to convict because of lack of evidence rather than lack of jurisdiction: "Why Pilate?" in Bammel, *Trial*, 78ff. It is often said on

the basis of the John text that the Synoptics suggest that the Sanhedrin could not impose the death sentence: for example, Catchpole in Bammel, *Trial*, 62.

36. For example, Mishnah Sanhedrin 11.2, Middoth, 5.4; Josephus *Jewish War* 5.144, 6.354; Tosefta Sanhedrin 7.1; Jerusalem Talmud 1 4 19c; Babylonian Talmud, Shabbath, 15a, Rosh Hashanah, 31a, Sanhedrin, 12a, 41a, 88b, Abodah Zarah, 8b.

37. Cf. Winter, *Trial*, 20, and the works he cites, 160 n. 2; Brown, *Death*, 1:348ff.

38. See, for example, D. R. Catchpole, "The Historicity of the Sanhedrin Trial," in Bammel, *Trial*, 58f.

39. See, for example, J. Duncan Derrett, *Law in the New Testament* (London, 1970), 160; also Shalom Albeck, "The Requirement of Two Witnesses in Jewish Law" in *Israeli Reports to the XIV International Congress of Comparative Law* (Jerusalem, 1994), 17ff.

40. See, for example, Brown, *Death*, 1:520ff., 1:532ff.

41. See, for example, Elias Bickerman, "Utilitas crucis," in *Studies in Jewish and Christian History* 3 (Leiden, 1986): 87.

42. See, for example, A. J. Saldanini in *The Anchor Bible Dictionary*, 5:978; Brown, *Death*, 1:343ff.

43. See, for example, Schürer, *History*, 2:210.

44. See, for example, Daube, *New Testament*, 303ff.

45. Cf. *The New Oxford Annotated Bible* (New York, 1991), 186 AP.

46. See also 2 Maccabees 8.4.

47. For our purposes we need not deal with the question that has troubled many commentators, whether the Sanhedrin operated in accordance with the law as interpreted by the Pharisees: cf. for example, Brown, *Death* 1:353ff. For us, it is enough that Jesus had also thoroughly incensed the Sadducees by his cleansing of the Temple; cf. Brown, *Death*, 1:361ff. For the charge see also J. C. O'Neill, "The Charge of Blasphemy at Jesus' Trial before the Sanhedrin," in Bammel, *Trial*, 72ff. For allegations of blasphemy at the trial see also Brown, *Death*, 1:534ff.

9 PONTIUS PILATE

1. For a discussion with reference to secondary sources see Brown, *Death*, 1:693ff.

2. For some who see Pilate as succumbing to Jewish pressure see Joel Carmichael, *The Death of Jesus* (London, 1963), 27; William R. Wilson, *The Execution of Jesus* (New York, 1970), 17ff.; Haim Cohn, *The Trial and Death of Jesus* (New York, 1971), 142ff.; Herman Hendrickx, *The Passion Narratives of the Synoptic Gospels* (Manila, 1977), 62ff.; Joseph B. Tyson, *The Death of Jesus in Luke-Acts* (Columbia, S.C., 1986), 136.

3. Exodus 20.2ff.; Deuteronomy 5.6ff.

4. Josephus *Jewish War* 2.169ff.; *Jewish Antiquities* 18.55ff.

5. *Jewish War* 2.175ff.

6. Mark 7.11; Matthew 15.5; cf. M. Wilcox in *Anchor Bible Dictionary*, 1:1134.

7. *Jewish Antiquities* 4.72f.

8. Ibid., 18.85ff.

9. *Embassy to Gaius* 301. Philo is discussing the episodes of the shields placed in Herod's palace.

10. Deuteronomy 12; cf. Deuteronomy 16.5f.

11. Josephus *Jewish Antiquities* 18.35, 18.95.

12. Ibid., 20.199ff.

13. Ibid., 15.403ff., 18.90ff., 20.6f.

14. Cf. Brown, *Death*, 1:335ff.

15. Cf. Winter, *Trial*, 91ff.

16. Alan Watson, *The Evolution of Law* (Baltimore, 1985), 43ff.

17. 14.12.22. A further fine example concerns the execution of Giorgio Scali in Niccolò Machiavelli *Istorie fiorentine* 3.20.

18. I am most indebted to the account in Winter, *Trial*, 91ff.: see also Brown, *Death*, 1:796ff., 1:811ff.

19. *Jewish Antiquities* 20:161; *Jewish War* 2:228, 253–54, 271; 4:198.

20. Mark 15.26; Matthew 27.37; Luke 23.37.

10 THE SLAVONIC JOSEPHUS

1. For the Slavonic Josephus, Robert Eisler is still fundamental: *The Messiah Jesus and John the Baptist*, 113ff. and passim; cf. Frederick J. Foakes-Jackson, *Josephus and the Jews* (London, 1930), 279ff.; Geoffrey A. Williamson, *The World of Josephus* (London, 1964), 309f.; S. G. F. Brandon, *Jesus and the Zealots* (Manchester, 1967), 364ff.

2. This is the translation—except that I have altered the sum back to 30 talents—given by Geoffrey A. Williamson, *Josephus: The Jewish War* (Harmondsworth, 1959), 404f. Other passages relevant to the New Testament appear on 401ff.

3. A. Rubinstein believes there is some evidence in the Slavonic Josephus that it goes back to a fuller Greek text than the one we have now: "Observations on the Old Russian Version of Josephus' *Wars*," *Journal of Semitic Studies* 2 (1957): 348.

4. Williamson, *Josephus*, 402; cf., for example, Brandon, *Jesus and the Zealots*, 366.

5. Williamson, *Josephus*, 402f. It should be noted, though, that despite Williamson's "unjustly condemned by Roman authority," in the text it is the Jews who execute Jesus.

6. See, for example, Brown, *Death*, 1:373f.

7. Origen, *Contra Celsum* 1.47; *Commentarius in Matthaeum* 13.55.

8. Eusebius *Historia Ecclesiae* 1.11. See Louis H. Feldman, *Josephus* (Cambridge, Mass., 1965), 9:49 n. 3.

9. Elias Bickerman does suggest that it was the translator into Slavonic who inserted the interpolations: "Sur la version vieux-russe de Flavius Josèphe," in *Studies in Jewish and Christian History* 3 (Leiden, 1986): 172ff. But this leaves inexplicable the resemblances between the Slavonic *Jewish War* and *Jewish Antiquities* 18:63f.

10. Certainly it appears subsequently that the handing over was to the soldiers.

11. Deuteronomy 21.1–9; Psalms 26.6, 73.13. Cf., for example, Cohn, *Trial and Death of Jesus*, 266f.; Brown, *Death*, 1:834.

12. Grant, *Historical Introduction*, 129f.; see also Dale C. Allison, *The New Moses: A Matthean Typology* (Minneapolis, 1993).

13. This is also in Mark 13.3. For Luke 21.37, Jesus bivouacked on the Mount of Olives.

11 JOHN: THE CORRECTIVE TO MARK

1. For a fuller account see Watson, *Jesus and the Jews*, 45ff.

2. Daube, *Collaboration with Tyranny in Rabbinic Law* (London, 1965); Daube, *Appeasement or Resistance* (Berkeley, 1987), 75ff., where he gives a synopsis and deals with Caiaphas.

3. Josephus *Jewish Antiquities* 18.302ff.

4. Cf. Daube, *Civil Disobedience*, 102.

5. Cf. Mann, *Mark*, 673ff.

6. Papias, as quoted by Eusebius *Historia Ecclesiae* 3.39.15; the Anti-Marcionite Prologue (quoted in Taylor, *Mark*, 3); Irenaeus *Adversus Haereticos* 3.1.2; Clement of Alexandria, as quoted by Eusebius *Historia Ecclesiae* 6.14.6f.; *Adumbrations* on 1 Peter v. 13); Origen, as quoted by Eusebius *Historia Ecclesiae* 6.25.5; Jerome *Commentarius in Matthaeum* proem 6.

7. Cf., for example, Taylor, *Mark*, 7f.; Cranfield, *Mark*, 5f. Not all scholars agree: see, for example, P. J. Achtemeier, in *The Anchor Bible Dictionary*, 4:542f.; C. S. Mann, *Mark*, 72ff., who regards it as derived, and in part conflated, from Matthew and Luke, 76f.

12 THE MESSIAH, THE SON OF DAVID

1. David Daube, "The Earliest Structure of the Gospels," *New Testament Studies* 5 (1958–1959): 180f.

2. Daube refers to Joshua ben Hananiah in Babylonian Talmud, Niddah, 696ff.

3. Daube refers to the famous Midrash of the four sons.

4. For the theological background to the question see Fitzmyer, *Luke X–XXIV*, 1299ff.

5. Taylor, *Mark*, 490.

6. Cranfield, *Mark*, 381f. The reference to Gagg is to R. P. Gagg, "Jesus und die Davidssohnfrage," *Theologische Zeitschrift* 7 (1951): 18ff.

7. Mann, *Mark*, 483.

8. In general for opinions held about the question see Fitzmyer, *Luke X–XXIV*, 1309ff.

9. That seems to be the sense of all three Synoptics. Moreover, David Daube has pointed out that in the Passover Haggadah, the first three questions are put by the sons, the fourth son is unable to put one, and the father or teacher provokes him into thinking: "Zukunftsmusik," *Bulletin of the John Rylands Library of Manchester* 68 (1985): 58ff.; cf. Calum M. Carmichael, "On Reading David Daube," in *Essays on Law and Religion: The Berkeley and Oxford Symposia in Honour of David Daube* (Berkeley, 1993), 44.

10. Matthew 1.18ff.; Luke 1.26ff., 3.23.

11. The tightness of the structure of the four questions suggests some degree of artificiality. Most likely there were several more questions, and the author of Mark has been selective.

12. See, for example, *The New Oxford Annotated Bible*, 160 NT; Johannes Munck, *The Acts of the Apostles* (Garden City, N.Y., 1967), xv.

13. See, for example, Munck, *Acts*, 18f.; Hans Conzelmann, *Acts of the Apostles*, 2d ed., trans. James Limburg et al. (Philadelphia, 1987), 20f.; Frederick F. Bruce, *The Acts of the Apostles* (Leicester, 1990), 126ff.

14. A standard interpretation is that in Psalm 110.1, David could not have been referring to himself because he did not arise from the dead, but is speaking specifically of the resurrection of Jesus who is the Messiah: see, for example, John W. Pecker, *Acts of the Apostles* (Cambridge, 1966), 30; William Neil, *The Acts of the Apostles* (London, 1973), 78; Ernest Haenchen, *The Acts of the Apostles: A Commentary*, trans. Bernard Noble et al. (Philadelphia, 1971), 182ff.; David John Williams, *Acts* (Peabody, Mass., 1985), 52. But nothing in Psalm 110.1 indicates that David was thinking of resurrection on earth, and that is not the way Jesus uses the text as recorded in the Gospels.

1. Cf. Brown, *Death*, 1:13ff.

2. See Daube, *New Testament*, 205ff.

3. Matthew and Luke play down Jesus' role in the confrontation: the scribes do say that he blasphemes. But their account, by an inconsistency, reveals the scribes had not spoken their thoughts.

4. See especially Mishnah Yoma 6.6f.

5. For a discussion of the concept of the Son of man see Brown, *Death*, 1:509.

6. See Watson, *Jesus and the Jews*, 39.

7. I accept the Markan tradition against that in John.

8. On these conditions of discipleship see Fitzmyer, *Luke X–XXIV*, 1059ff.

9. Mark 13.9ff.; Matthew 24.9ff.; Luke 21.12ff.

10. Mark 14.31; Matthew 26.35; Luke 22.33.

11. Mark 14.47; Matthew 26.51; Luke 22.35ff., 22.50.

12. Cf. Brown, *Death*, 1:473ff.

13. For details see Daube, *New Testament*, 332ff.

14. David Daube, "A Prayer Pattern in Judaism," *Studia Evangelica* 73 (1959): 539ff.

15. For the confession of sin of one about to be stoned, and especially of one about to be stoned because of false witness, see Mishnah Sanhedrin 6.2; cf. Daube, "Prayer Pattern," 541.

16. See Daube, *Civil Disobedience*, 101ff.

17. See Mishnah Shekalim 1.3.

18. Cf., for example, Sanders, *Jewish Law*, 49.

19. Mishnah Zebahim.

20. See, for example, Deuteronomy 17.1.

21. Mishnah Shekalim 6.5; cf. Strack-Billerbeck, *Kommentar*, 1:850.

22. But see the explanation in Daube, *Civil Disobedience*, 106f., that Jesus was enraged by "the visible, tangible disturbance of the ideal sacred atmosphere." Daube correctly observed that the physical violence was directed against small folk.

23. *Jewish Antiquities* 18.17.

24. See, for example, Exodus 28–29; Numbers 5.11–31, 16–18; Leviticus 13–14; Deuteronomy 24.8f.; cf. for example, Schürer, *History*, 2:238ff.

25. Oddly, Albright and Mann think the incident would not have attracted much attention; *Matthew*, 254f. They also stress that money changing would be a lucrative privilege, and they virtually ignore the religious implications for the Jews of Jesus' behavior. But this is frequent among Christian scholars. For instance, for Fitzmyer, Jesus proceeds to the "Temple and in a prophetic act purges it of those who by their mercantile traffic were profaning its character as a house of prayer": *Luke X–XXIV*, 1260.

26. Sanders, *Jewish Law*, 2.

27. For this parable and its appearance in the Gospel of Thomas see Fitzmyer, *Luke X–XXIV*, 1277ff.

28. *Jewish War* 2.125; cf. Brown, *Death*, 1:268f.

29. See Brown, *Death*, 1:435f.

30. Cf., for example, Brandon, *Jesus and the Zealots*, 251ff.

31. Brown, for example, misses the point: *Death*, 1:517ff.

32. See, for example, Josephus *Jewish Antiquities* 20.200; Acts 6.12ff., 7.1ff., 57ff. The contrary claim in John 18.31 is one of the ways in which the redactor shows his ignorance of Judaism.

33. In fact it was widespread, though underplayed, in the tradition that Jesus was not condemned by the Sanhedrin. Thus, we find in Acts 13.28: "Even though they [the residents of Jerusalem and their leaders: Acts 3.27] found no cause for a sentence of death, they asked Pilate to have him killed." I accept the standard view that Acts was written by the author of Luke. The account of the Sanhedrin proceedings and their aftermath is confused in Luke, but in Acts this is explicit. There was a strong strand in the tradition that insisted Jesus was not condemned by the Sanhedrin: see also the appendix.

34. For skillful use of formalities by a trickster to achieve a hidden end where the narrative shows clear awareness of the trick see Daube, *Studies in Biblical Law*, 190ff.

35. Sherwin-White, *Roman Society*, 32f.

36. If we accept that there is a historical element in the episode, then the timing is that of Matthew. Jesus' words in Luke 13.35 are incomprehensible for that time.

37. Rudolf Otto, *The Kingdom of God and the Son of Man*, trans. F. V. Filson and B. L. Woolf (London, 1938), 361f.; cf. Taylor, *Mark*, 402.

38. Cf. Matthew 24.46. For a full discussion of views that have been held, see Brown, *Death*, 2:1044.

✠

INDEX OF TEXTS

✠ ✠ ✠

1 OLD TESTAMENT

207

4 RABBINIC AND OTHER JEWISH SOURCES

PHILO
Embassy to Gaius

5 CLASSICAL SOURCES